INTERMEDIATE PORTUGUESE SHORT STORIES

10 Captivating Short Stories to Learn Brazilian Portuguese & Grow Your Vocabulary the Fun Way!

Intermediate Portuguese Stories

www.LingoMastery.com

ISBN: 9781689542241

CONTENTS

INTRODUCTION

So, you want to improve your Portuguese? That's awesome, reader! Portuguese is a beautiful language spoken by over 250 million people across the world, being the mother tongue in amazing countries, such as Brazil, Portugal, Cape Verde, etc., and even in Macau, a city in China! It is a language that has spread across every continent and which opens the doors to entire worlds once you learn how to speak it.

Portuguese is a very old language, and its written form can be dated back to the 12th century. Vulgar Latin, which was spoken on the west coast of the Iberian Peninsula, (now Portugal and the Spanish province of Galicia) basically replaced all previous local languages. Vulgar Latin evolved into the Galician–Portuguese language. This then broke off into Galician and Portuguese after the incorporation of Galicia into Spain and the independent development of Portugal.

It may be important to note at this point that having an intermediate level of Portuguese may be an important tool for your professional future, as well as opening several doors for you on your resume if you feel the need to either migrate or work in a multi-cultural environment. Portuguese speakers will usually appreciate your effort in having partially or fully learned their language, and they will happily collaborate with you in solving your doubts.

What the following book is about

We've written this book to cover an important issue that seems to affect every new learner of the Portuguese language — a lack of helpful reading material. While in English you may encounter tons (or gigabytes, in our modern terms) of easy and accessible learning material, in Portuguese you will usually and promptly be given tough literature to read by your teachers, and you will soon find yourself consulting your dictionary more than you'd want to. Eventually, you'll find yourself bored and uninterested in continuing, and your initially positive outlook may soon turn sour.

There's something you must understand: Portuguese isn't an easy language, but it isn't a horribly difficult one either. You just need to make an effort in identifying your flaws and weaknesses and having purchased this book is a definite good start.

Our goal with this book will be to supply you with useful, entertaining, helpful and challenging material that will not only allow you to learn the language but also help you pass the time and make the experience less formal and more fun — like any particular lesson should be. We will not bore you with grammatical notes, spelling or structure: the book has been well-written and revised to ensure that it covers those aspects without having to explain them in unnecessarily complicated rules like textbooks do.

If you've ever learned a new language through conversational methods, teachers will typically just ask you to practice speaking. Here, we'll teach you writing and reading Portuguese with stories. You'll both learn how to read it *and* write it with the additional tools we'll give you at the end of each story.

How *Intermediate Portuguese Short Stories* has been laid out

We want to help you read stories and understand each aspect of the language in the most entertaining way, so we've compiled a series of tales which will each cover a tool of the language. Each story will tell a different tale involving unique, deep characters with their own personalities and conflicts, while ensuring that you understand the objective of the language device in Portuguese. Conjugation, Comparisons, Tenses, Passive and Active and more will be covered in this Intermediate-level book. At no point will we introduce concepts too difficult for you to grasp, and any complicated vocabulary will be studied at the end of each story.

The stories have been written in a way that will allow you to:

a) Read the story without any distractions, paying attention solely to the plot of the tale without making special emphasis on distracting elements.

b) Interpret the tale you just read with the use of two summaries — one in English so that you may ensure you understood what the tale was about and can go back to it if there was something you didn't understand properly; and another in Portuguese for when you start to dominate the language a bit better, allowing you to create your own summary for the book later on.

c) Understand the related terms expressed throughout the story with the use of a list of vocabulary that will give you important definitions and clear up any doubts you may have acquired.

d) Finally: ensure you have understood what you've read by providing you with a list of simple-choice questions based on the story, with a list of answers below if you want to corroborate your choices.

All of this will ensure absolute efficiency in not only reading the stories, but in understanding and interpreting them once you're done. It is normal that you may find certain terms unknown to your knowledge of the language, and it is equally normal that sometimes you may ultimately not entirely understand what the story is about. We're here to *help* you, in any way we can.

Recommendations for readers of *Intermediate Portuguese Short Stories*

Before we allow you to begin reading, we have a quick list of recommendations, tips and tricks for getting the best out of this book.

1. Read the stories without any pressure: feel free to return to parts you didn't understand and take breaks when necessary. This is like any fantasy, romance or sci-fi book you'd pick up, except with different goals.
2. Feel free to use any external material to make your experience more complete: while we've provided you with plenty of data to help you learn, you may feel obliged to look at textbooks or search for more helpful texts on the internet — do not think twice about doing so! We even recommend it.
3. Find other people to learn with: while learning can be fun on your own, it helps to have friends or family joining you on the tough journey of learning a new language. Find a like-minded person to accompany you in this experience, and you may soon find yourself competing to see who can learn the most!
4. Try writing your own stories once you're done: all the material in this book is made for you to learn not only how to read, but how to write as well. Liked what you read? Try writing your own story now, and see what people think about it!

Well, with all of that said, we can finally begin with the book — after all, we want you to start reading our stories right away.

FREE BOOK!

Free Book Reveals The 6 Step Blueprint That Took Students

From Language Learners To Fluent In 3 Months

One last thing before we start. If you haven't already, head over to LingoMastery.com/hacks and grab a copy of our free Lingo Hacks book that will teach you the important secrets that you need to know to become fluent in a language as fast as possible.

Now, without further ado, enjoy these 10 Portuguese Stories for Intermediate learners.

CHAPTER ONE

INTERMEDIATE VOCABULARY AND SUPERLATIVES

Entre cem restaurantes, apenas um me agrada – Among a hundred restaurants, only one pleases me

Quando ainda jovem adorava ir a vários restaurantes pela minha **cidade natal**. A pesar de ser localizada em um **município** longe da **metrópole** em que hoje resido, a variedade **gastronômica** era **impressionante**, o turismo ajudava muito a manter todos esses restaurantes abertos ou muitas vezes a **redecorá-los** durante toda **temporada** ou datas festivas.

Meus pais eram professores, dois **amantes** da leitura, sempre em busca de novos **conhecimentos**. Dona Marisa, minha mãe, **lecionava** a matéria de história e estava sempre disposta a desbravar novos horizontes. Lembro-me de nossa viagem à cidade de Betim, histórica e **pacata** cidade ao lado da nossa, e de uma conversa em particular; eu tinha apenas 15 anos.

- Veja Benjamin, em Betim há a cultura de curar e criar **queijos** dos mais diversos modos e saborosíssimos, quanto mais andarmos pela cidade mais fatos curiosos encontraremos. - disse minha mãe.

- Sim, mãe, podemos ir a algum restaurante típico da cidade? - perguntei a ela.

- Claro, iremos **almoçar** no **famosíssimo** Mandacaru, conhecido por seus pratos exóticos, como a **linguiça** temperada, farofa com queijo coalho. Vamos adorar! - respondeu minha saudosíssima mãe.

Naquele dia, realmente conhecemos um dos restaurantes mais deliciosos em que já estive. Saboreei cada pedaço de minha **refeição**, mas, ao mesmo tempo, notei algumas pessoas **animadíssimas** que estavam no local; comiam a refeição com muita calma e observavam tudo ao seu redor.

Um dia depois descobri que eram **críticos** de gastronomia. Suas anotações e observações estavam em uma matéria do jornal local; elogiaram a comida, mas se queixaram do serviço e do **vinho**. Perguntei ao meu pai o que faziam aquelas pessoas, pois havia fotos de seus rostos no canto da matéria.

- Eles têm como profissão conhecer novos restaurantes e avaliar todo o seu serviço, assim como a comida oferecida pelo **estabelecimento** e em sua maioria são **jornalistas** com máximo conhecimento dedicado à gastronomia. Você seria um excelente crítico gastronômico, meu filho!! - respondeu meu pai.

Nossa, eu adorei essa **profissão**. Como posso me tornar um, vou investigar... - Falei alto na mesa do café da manhã e meus pais riram e me deram todo o apoio necessário.

Quando retornei à minha cidade, comecei a olhar os restaurantes de um novo jeito. Analisava desde a fachada do local até se o **guardanapo** era de papel ou pano. Passei a me ver como crítico da cidade e a explanar minhas opiniões acerca dos locais visitados.

Com o passar dos anos, resolvi **ingressar** na faculdade de jornalismo e profissionalizar o serviço que eu adorava prestar: criticar, criticar e criticar mais um pouco - pelo ponto de vista positivo, que fique claro.

Na mudança para a capital conheci um novo mundo onde a diversidade oferecida era ainda maior. Se eu pudesse, conseguiria lanchar, almoçar e jantar em locais diferentes todos os dias.

Voltando ao plano de **carreira**. Para ser crítico gastronômico iniciei a tarefa **dificílima** de desbravar os locais mais inusitados da cidade, pois, no meu pensamento, os lugares **chiques** e abertos recentemente já seriam visitados por críticos mais famosos e conhecidos do ramo. Montei um plano para conhecer cem restaurantes diferentes em seis meses, com preços diversos e ambientes mais diversos ainda.

Conversei com um dos professores da universidade que achou a ideia criativa e **ousadíssima**, contei a meus pais que adoraram e se prontificaram a me visitar e conhecer alguns deles comigo. Nessa etapa, estava empolgadíssimo e criei com a ajuda de uma amiga próxima um site onde pude compartilhar todos os conteúdos, fotos e notas para os critérios de avaliação criados por mim.

Bom, o projeto precisava de um nome **impactante** e que chamasse a atenção, pois a ideia era transformar isso numa profissão. Como não consegui pensar em um nome sozinho fui conversar com dois colegas da faculdade, Paulo e Jorge.

- Ben, o nome pode ser "100 lugares com emoção"? "**Roteiro** de lugares inusitados"?

- Estou menos **criativo** hoje. Vou pensar um pouco. - disse Paulo.

- Ah, você poderia chamar de "Projeto Ben - 100 lugares para conhecer", o que acha? - disse Jorge.

- Poxa, achei pouco impactante. O que acham de "Os **melhores** dos cem melhores"? "Onde comer em Sampa"? "Os cem do Ben"? - respondi para eles.

- Eu gostei de "Os cem do Ben", o que acha Paulo? - disse Jorge.

- Curtidíssimo! Onde eu acompanho as notícias mesmo? - Paulo respondeu rindo, mas sabendo que aquele era o nome certo.

Essa conversa aconteceu numa sexta-feira; no domingo à tarde o site já estava pronto. Eu me organizei para começar as **visitações** na semana seguinte, pois teria tempo hábil para ajustar qualquer problema técnico, e fiz até um curso rápido de **fotografia** para ter fotos atraentes e com um certo **talento**.

Para conseguir apreciar o café da manhã de algumas padarias próximas à minha casa, fiz algumas **caminhadas** e fui anotando todas as que julgava divertidas, conceituais e que mereciam a minha visita. Comprei três camisetas e três calças jeans iguais, como uma espécie de uniforme extraoficial, achei que traria mais **profissionalismo** para o projeto. Estava **felicíssimo** e empolgadíssimo.

É chegada a hora de iniciar meu projeto, sobre o qual já havia feito uma enorme **propaganda** na faculdade, no prédio onde residia, nas redes sociais, e por isso esperava que ao menos os meus amigos visitassem o site e deixassem suas opiniões **sinceras**.

Nas duas primeiras semanas planejei dar mais atenção para os cafés da manhã, claro que eu estava alternando os dias de visita, não tinha dinheiro para comer fora todos os dias. A primeira padaria que visitei ficava próxima do meu apartamento, a apenas duas quadras. Após uma caminhada **rápida** cheguei ao local e perguntei se podia fazer fotos da minha refeição e pedi autorização aos responsáveis para publicá-las. Fui **negado**!

Fiquei chateado, mas sabia que isso poderia acontecer. Sendo assim, fui até à próxima da lista e lá fui muito bem recebido. Perguntaram se eu era blogueiro e respondi que era apenas um curioso - não quis dar muitos detalhes, pois o **comportamento** dos funcionários poderia não ser verdadeiro.

O serviço em si foi **boníssimo**; a comida, um pouco fria. Mesmo assim, o **gosto** estava muito bom. Fiz todo o processo das fotos da refeição, que custou muito pouco em comparação ao local anterior que **recusara** a autorização para as fotos. Corri para casa e iniciei o processo de escrita e diagramação, novamente **empolgadíssimo**. De tarde consegui fazer a minha primeira postagem, divulguei para todos, comuniquei ao pessoal da faculdade em nossos grupos nas redes sociais.

"Boa tarde amigos, é com um prazer inenarrável (as pessoas sempre acharam engraçado esse meu jeito superlativo de falar e escrever, mas eu adoro) e muita empolgação que comunico a primeira publicação do projeto "Os cem do Ben". Apreciem e, se gostarem, compartilhem o meu conteúdo, e se não gostarem me digam o que pode melhorar. Até mais pessoal" - publiquei para todos.

As visitações no primeiro dia não foram muito altas, mas eu não desisti: falava com todos e anunciava sempre em minhas redes sociais, comecei a **frequentar** mais padarias e lugares para café da manhã. Recebi até alguns **recados** dos próprios proprietários em agradecimento às postagens e sugestões feitas; como o da lanchonete *Leve Mais*, onde pude notar com certo estranhamento que a televisão do saguão ficava passando vídeos de música, mas sem som, ou seja, somente os cantores parecendo serem **mudos.** Sugeri programas que não necessitavam de áudio para melhorar a harmonia do lugar. A sugestão foi acatada e notada por outros **clientes**. Fiquei muito feliz, até ganhei um café completo de brinde.

Quando iniciei a temporada de almoços o site já estava com um número maior de **visualizações** e comentários, todos **ansiosíssimos** pelas indicações de restaurantes. Visitei vários locais com diversas especialidades: comida japonesa, brasileira, italiana, contemporânea... Uns com preços baixos, outros com valores mais elevados, enfim, fiz uma temporada brilhante e muito elogiada.

Em um domingo enquanto revisava uma das minhas **publicações,** notei que ainda não tinha visitado um restaurante onde não houvesse do que reclamar ou sugerir melhorias. Fiquei espantado, achei que estava crítico em demasia. Em uma das minhas postagens percebi que pessoas conhecidas estavam notando e elogiando a existência do meu projeto, nomes os quais eu acompanhava de perto.

Ao analisar as resenhas dessas personalidades pude notar que elas também criticavam e sugeriam bastante, até mesmo aqueles restaurantes conceituadíssimos. Fiquei mais calmo e prossegui para a temporada de jantares (confesso que o mais pedido pelos comentaristas **recorrentes**.)

Ao entrar em um dos restaurantes em minha lista fui reconhecido pelo gerente do local que apesar de **educadíssimo** não liberou que as fotos fossem tiradas e pediu que nenhum conteúdo fosse feito. Como estava com mais um amigo decidimos ir embora e buscar um novo local para conhecer. Andamos cerca de três quadras e notamos um pequeno bistrô no final de uma rua.

- Olha Jorge, acho que aquele ali pode valer a pena. - disse para Jorge.

- Ben, o lugar é muito bonito e o nome também é sugestivo, Magali Bistrô. - respondeu Jorge.

Entramos no local e fui surpreendido por uma moça muito simpática e educadíssima. **Notamos** que a comida servida era autoral e possuía uma mistura de culinária nordestina com paulista. O serviço da casa era excelente, obtivemos a autorização para as fotos e nada saiu do lugar; eu não conseguia achar nada para criticar negativamente ou sugerir mudanças. Como eu estava feliz! Aquele era o restaurante da minha vida.

O projeto foi encerrado e deu lugar a uma **coluna** permanente em um **jornal** local, pois havia sido um sucesso. As críticas eram disponibilizadas em papel e pela Internet. Quando eu percebi, tinha me tornando aquele crítico gastronômico dos meus sonhos.

Resumo da história

Quantos de nós sabemos nossa vocação profissional desde pequenos? Com Ben, não foi diferente! Após uma experiência em Betim acompanhado por seus pais, o garoto resolve se dedicar à carreira de crítico gastronômico, e conhece o sucesso ao assumir o risco de colocar em prática um projeto experimental que envolveu bastante esforço pessoal e a ajuda de seus colegas.

Summary of the story

How many of us have the feeling to know our professional vocation since we were little? With Ben, it was no different! After an experience in the city of Betim accompanied by his parents, the boy decides to dedicate himself to the career of gastronomic critic. He achieves success after taking the risk of putting into practice an experimental project that involved a lot of personal effort and the help of his colleagues.

Vocabulary

- **quando:** when
- **cidade natal:** hometown
- **município:** city
- **metrópole:** metropolis
- **gastronômica:** gastronomic
- **impressionante:** impressive
- **redecorar:** redecorate
- **temporada:** season
- **amantes:** lovers
- **conhecimentos:** knowledge
- **lecionava:** taught
- **pacata:** calm
- **queijos:** cheese
- **almoçar:** to have lunch
- **famosíssimo:** very famous
- **linguiça:** sausage
- **refeição:** meal
- **animadíssimas:** very excited
- **críticos:** critics
- **vinho:** wine
- **estabelecimento:** establishment
- **jornalistas:** journalists
- **profissão:** occupation
- **guardanapo:** napkin
- **carreira:** career
- **dificílima:** very hard
- **chiques:** fancy
- **ousadíssima:** very daring
- **impactante:** shocking
- **roteiro:** script
- **criativo:** creative
- **melhores:** the best
- **visitações:** visits
- **fotografia:** photography
- **talento:** talent
- **caminhadas:** walks
- **profissionalismo:** professionalism
- **felicíssimo:** very happy
- **propaganda:** advertisement
- **sinceras:** sincere
- **rápida:** fast
- **negado:** denied
- **comportamento:** behavior
- **boníssimo:** very good
- **gosto:** taste
- **recusara:** refused
- **empolgadíssimo:** very excited

- **frequentar:** to attend
- **recados:** messages
- **mudos:** mute
- **clientes:** clients
- **visualizações:** views
- **ansiosíssimos:** very anxious
- **publicações:** posts
- **recorrentes:** recurrent
- **educadíssimo:** very polite
- **notamos:** we noticed
- **coluna:** column (periodical)
- **jornal:** newspaper

Questions about the story

1. **Qual a profissão dos pais de Ben?**

   a) Professores
   b) Agricultores
   c) Engenheiros
   d) Médicos

2. **Qual cidade Ben visitou quando decidiu se tornar um crítico?**

   a) Tiradentes
   b) São Paulo
   c) Betim
   d) Rio de Janeiro

3. **Com qual refeição Ben iniciou seu projeto?**

   a) Café da manhã
   b) Jantar
   c) Almoço
   d) Ceia

4. **Qual foi o nome escolhido para o projeto?**

   a) 100 lugares para conhecer
   b) Os 100 do Ben
   c) Onde comer em Sampa?
   d) Os melhores dos cem melhores

5. **Qual restaurante Ben não teve nenhuma crítica a fazer?**

   a) Restaurante Betim
   b) Cozinha Italiana
   c) Leve Mais
   d) Magali Bistrô

Answers

1. A
2. C
3. A
4. B
5. D

CHAPTER TWO

IMPERFECT

O amado bairro de São Jorge – The beloved neighborhood of São Jorge

Que saudade da **época** em que morava no **magnífico** bairro de São Jorge! Quando era **criança** achava que moraria ali para o resto da minha vida. **Antigamente**, tudo acontecia naquele **bairro**, existiam ruas com muitos bares famosos como o Bar do Juquinha; essa rua sei que ainda existe, mas se tornou mais boêmia e saudosista.

Eu morava próximo à Praça de Hércules. O nome foi dado devido ao **fundador** da cidade, um historiador **famoso** por ser forte e aguentar qualquer problema. Dizem que ele adorava se exercitar onde hoje é a **praça**. Quando o bairro começou a crescer deram este nome em sua **homenagem**. Todos os dias após a escola nos encontrávamos na praça para jogar futebol ou ficar conversando sobre a vida.

Morei no bairro até meus vinte e quatro anos, eu **estudava** no colégio São Jorge I, todos nos conheciam, era ótimo, os professores eram como nossos amigos. Brinco com meus filhos que hoje eles não sabem o que é ser chamado pelo primeiro nome pela **diretora** da escola mesmo que seja para levar uma **bronca.**

Na minha época quem comandava o colégio era a Dona Célia, uma mulher alta de cabelos loiros que fazia de tudo para ser **respeitada** pelos alunos. No entanto, ela era muito simpática, às vezes até esquecíamos que era nossa diretora. Ao passear pelo bairro hoje

reconheci a Dona Célia em uma **cadeira** ao lado de fora de sua casa e parei para ver se ela me reconheceria.

- Olá, dona Célia! Como está a senhora? - disse superanimado para ela.

- Rafael Menezes, que saudade! Estou ótima, e com muito calor nesse São Jorge, por isso estou aqui fora. Ano passado não fez tanto calor assim. E você, como está? - disse Dona Célia.

Por um instante, fiquei **observando** emocionado como ela ainda se lembrava de mim, como era **gratificante** estar ali conversando com ela.

- Que bom que lembrou de mim, que emoção, minha querida diretora. Sou **casado**, moro em Limeira, com minha esposa e filho (Danilo), estou muito bem, **visitando** minha mãe Joana que ainda mora ali na Rua Castro e Silva. - respondi para ela.

- Claro! Sua mãe é muito querida, eu sentia o **cheiro** dos bolos de laranja de longe ao passar pela rua onde ela mora. Todas as vezes em que a encontro nos **lembramos** da época em que você aprontava no São Jorge I. Você está lembrado de quando matou aula para ficar a manhã toda comendo jabuticaba nos fundos do colégio, mas teve que **implorar** para o porteiro te deixar entrar pois estava com dor de barriga? - Dona Célia começa a **rir** de mim.

- Lembro, lembro. Meu **parceiro** Silvio saiu correndo para casa dele e me deixou lá **sozinho**! Aquele cara era muito **engraçado**. Tem notícias dele? Nunca mais o vi. - respondi para Dona Célia.

- Sim, meu filho, Silvinho já faleceu. **Infelizmente** o coração dele não estava funcionando muito bem, já faz dez anos que ele se foi, deixou um filho pequeno na época, o Silvio Filho.

- Nossa, minha mãe deve ter esquecido de avisar. Lembro-me que fazia algum tempo que ele estava com a **saúde** debilitada, mas não sabia que era ruim assim. - Respondi para Dona Célia com um **olhar triste**, pois não sabia da morte de Silvio e nem que fazia tanto tempo assim.

Ao me **despedir** de Dona Célia, algumas **lágrimas** caíram de meu olho e pude notar que estava muito saudoso naquele dia. Ela riu de mim e me deu um **abraço** bem apertado e disse que se orgulhava do homem que eu havia me tornado e que **perdoava** todas as minhas maluquices da época escolar.

Caminhando para a casa de minha mãe encontro o Zé, dono da mercearia do bairro, onde trabalhava nas férias **limpando** a calçada da loja para ganhar um dinheiro extra. Assim que nossos rostos se encontram ele **grita** bem alto para mim:

- Veja se não é o melhor limpador de calçada do bairro, Rafinha, o **terrível**!!

- Opa, opa! Olha se não é o melhor comerciante desse bairro, o Zé da goiaba!! - grito de volta para ele.

- Como você está, Rafinha? E o filhão, trouxe para o pessoal conhecer? Entre e beba um refrigerante conosco. – Ele disse.

Ao entrar na loja muitas **recordações** aparecem, alguns funcionários continuam os mesmos, mas também vejo rostos novos. O chão foi mudado, agora está mais fácil de limpar. Na minha época demorava uma manhã inteira para limpar o chão da **calçada**. Agora, é só passar uma vassoura e está tudo certo.

- Zé, meu filho não pôde vir, está cheio de atividades no colégio, ficou em casa com minha **esposa**. Que bom te ver! Como vão Márcia, Tiago... enfim, todos os seus filhos. - Respondo para o Zé enquanto sentamos em uma mesa para clientes na lanchonete da mercearia.

- Os meninos estão ótimos, a Márcia está finalizando a faculdade de Medicina, Tiago trabalha aqui no comércio comigo. Estão todos felizes. Ainda não tenho **netos**, mas já ando cobrando deles. - disse Zé.

Quando converso com o Zé perco a **noção do tempo.** Passei mais de uma hora conversando com o primeiro chefe que tive na vida, pessoa pela qual sempre terei muito apreço e **respeito**. Ao perceber o quanto havia se passado e que o refrigerante já havia acabado fazia algum tempo, levanto da cadeira e me despeço de todos e de Zé, meu querido amigo, muito amigo também de meu **falecido** pai, de quem ele sempre relembra momentos bons.

Quando chego na casa de minha mãe penso em Dona Célia, pois o cheiro de bolo de laranja estava por toda parte. Era delicioso. Eu falava desse bolo para todos na escola, sempre levava um pedaço para minha **namorada** da época, a Marcela.

Lembrei que ela ainda morava no bairro, havia se casado com o Rodrigo e era advogada. Como eu sempre fui muito feliz por todas as suas conquistas, minha esposa tinha muito ciúme. Marcela sempre foi muito bonita, igual a essas modelos que vemos na televisão. Pergunto sobre ela para minha mãe.

- Mãe, você tem notícias de Marcela? Como ela está? Hoje estou saudosista. - pergunto para Dona Maria.

- Meu filho, ela está ótima. Fazia tempo que eu não lembrava de Marcela. A última vez que a vi foi no salão de festas na quermesse da **igreja**, linda como sempre e hoje tem dois filhos. - diz minha mãe.

- Ótimo, fico feliz! - respondo.

Terminamos nosso namoro porque fui **aprovado** em uma universidade na capital com bolsa integral e ela não quis deixar São Jorge, além disso, já fazia algum tempo que não estávamos bem. Acho que foi o melhor para os dois.

Sento-me à mesa que a minha mãe fez questão de arrumar para o café da tarde, tudo muito farto como costumávamos fazer quando ainda morava ali. Sirvo uma xícara de café para cada e dona Maria corta o **bolo** que ainda estava um pouco quente, mas aparentava estar delicioso; comia sempre que ela fazia e nunca sobrava por muitos dias.

A casa de minha mãe não mudou muita coisa, ela vivia ali com minha **sobrinha** que era professora justamente do colégio São Jorge I. Era bom pois ela fazia companhia para minha mãe que já tinha seus 77 anos. O meu quarto havia virado uma espécie de quarto de **costura** onde mamãe fingia que costurava cortinas para a casa - nunca vi uma peça pronta, mas tudo bem.

O **quintal** também me trazia ótimas lembranças; eu e minha **irmã** fomos muito felizes naquele lugar. Que saudade da minha infância! Sempre que posso vou até o bairro para visitar a todos. Gosto muito do ambiente, os pés de jabuticaba ainda estão lá atrás do colégio, as mangueiras decoram a Rua Vinte de Maio e alimentam os pássaros que sempre aparecem nos finais de tarde. O ar de bairro familiar ainda suspira por São Jorge.

Ao sair na rua novamente vejo uma placa de anúncio de venda da casa de Dona Amélia que infelizmente havia falecido e não teve filhos durante a vida. Num impulso, vou verificar as condições da casa e qual valor pedido. Para meu **espanto,** a casa mantém a arquitetura original e poucas coisas devem ser ajustadas; os vizinhos são todos conhecidos e amigáveis; a **oportunidade** está diante de mim.

- São Jorge, estou voltando!! O que acha minha mãe? - pergunto.

- **Maravilhoso**, meu filho! Será um prazer ter você novamente morando em nosso bairro. Podemos fazer as nossas antigas festas juninas, ver os meninos pulando carnaval na rua, Danilo poderia estudar onde você estudou! Ia ser muito bom! - disse ela.

- Seria um sonho, minha mãe! - respondo com o maior sorriso no rosto.

Resumo da história

Em uma visita a seu antigo bairro, Rafael reencontra velhos companheiros de juventude, como a diretora de sua escola e seu primeiro chefe. Nessa jornada nostálgica, acaba descobrindo que há uma casa à venda nesse local que tanto marcou seus primeiros passos. Seria essa a oportunidade perfeita para proporcionar a seu filho tudo o que ele havia vivido um dia?

Summary of the story

In a visit to his old neighborhood, Rafael finds his old friends, like the director of his school and his first boss. On this nostalgic journey, he discovers that there is a house for sale in this place that has marked his first steps. Would that be the perfect opportunity to give his son everything he had once experienced?

Vocabulary

- **época:** time
- **magnífico:** magnificent
- **criança:** child
- **antigamente:** in the old days
- **bairro:** neighborhood
- **fundador:** founder
- **famoso:** famous
- **praça:** square
- **homenagem:** tribute
- **estudava:** studied
- **diretora:** principal
- **bronca:** reprimand
- **respeitada:** respected
- **reconheci:** recognized
- **cadeira:** chair
- **observando:** observing
- **gratificante:** gratifying
- **casado:** married
- **visitando:** visiting
- **cheiro:** smell
- **lembramos:** we remembered
- **implorar:** to beg
- **rir:** to laugh
- **parceiro:** partner
- **sozinho:** alone
- **engraçado:** funny
- **infelizmente:** unfortunately
- **saúde:** health
- **olhar triste:** sad look
- **despedir:** to say goodbye
- **lágrimas:** tears
- **abraço:** hug
- **perdoava:** forgive
- **limpando:** cleaning
- **grita:** yell
- **terrível:** terrific
- **recordações:** memories
- **calçada:** sidewalk
- **esposa:** wife
- **netos:** grandchildren
- **noção do tempo:** sense of time
- **respeito:** respect
- **falecido:** deceased
- **namorada:** girlfriend
- **igreja:** church
- **aprovado:** approved
- **bolo:** cake
- **sobrinha:** niece
- **costura:** seam
- **quintal:** yard
- **irmã:** sister
- **espanto:** astonishment
- **oportunidade:** opportunity
- **maravilhoso:** wonderful

Questions about the story

1. **De qual bairro Rafael sente saudade?**

   a) São Jorge
   b) Bom Retiro
   c) Copacabana
   d) Leblon

2. **Quem é Dona Célia?**

   a) Sua mãe
   b) Sua antiga namorada
   c) A diretora de sua escola
   d) Sua atual esposa

3. **Quem foi o primeiro chefe de Rafael?**

   a) Carlos
   b) Silvinho
   c) Rafinha
   d) Zé

4. **Quem são Márcia e Tiago?**

   a) Netos do Zé
   b) Filhos do Zé
   c) Parentes de Dona Célia
   d) Filhos de Rafael

5. **Por que Rafael e Marcela se separaram?**

   a) Rafael entrou na universidade
   b) Rafael arranjou um emprego novo
   c) Marcela conheceu outro rapaz
   d) Marcela mudou de cidade

Answers

1. A
2. C
3. D
4. B
5. A

CHAPTER THREE

FUTURE PERFECT

Rumo à maratona! – Towards the marathon!

Meu nome é Joana, tenho 34 anos, sou **professora de inglês**, **costureira**, animadora de festa, tenho dois filhos e estou recém **divorciada**. Minha vida está **completamente** diferente do que era há um ano **atrás**. Nos últimos meses acabei deixando a **vaidade** um pouco a desejar.

Sempre fui aquela mulher que escovava os cabelos, costurava roupas novas para mim, andava com a **maquiagem** maravilhosa, mas após o divórcio comecei a duvidar de mim mesma e a deixar de ser vaidosa. Resultado: dez quilos a mais na **balança**!

Hoje resolvi tomar uma **atitude**. Irei ao médico para verificar minha saúde e também ao **nutricionista**, pois preciso **emagrecer** e cuidar mais de mim. Eu falarei com a minha irmã para ajudar na questão da vaidade e **marcarei** agora as consultas.

- Boa tarde, gostaria de marcar uma **consulta** com a nutricionista. - Ligo para a clínica de minha amiga que sei que irá me ajudar.

- Claro, temos uma vaga para **amanhã** às 14h (quatorze horas). Está bom para a senhorita? - disse a telefonista.

Adorei ser chamada de senhorita, já comecei gostando da **clínica**. Afinal, agora farei de tudo para voltar a ser saudável e atlética.

- Sim, está ótimo. - respondo.

- Seu **nome completo** e telefone, por favor. - pergunta a telefonista.

- Joana Ribeiro Alves... digo, Joana Ribeiro Lima, meu nome de solteira! Me consultarei com qual doutor? - respondo rindo para a telefonista.

- Com a Doutora Márcia; está **confirmada** a sua consulta. Esperarei pela senhorita amanhã. Boa tarde. - responde a telefonista.

- Boa tarde. **Até amanhã**!

Quando chego na consulta, percebo que deixarei de tomar **refrigerante** por um bom tempo, então, como ainda estou adiantada, resolvo ir até à **lanchonete** ao lado da clínica para tomar minha última **lata** de refrigerante, pois tenho certeza que serei **proibida** de fazê-lo. Ao terminar de beber, percebo que estou parecendo uma criança, ansiosa para chegar a hora da festa. Estou de fato muito **animada**.

Ao entrar no consultório e perceber que a nutricionista é extremamente **simpática** e **receptiva**, sinto que farei um excelente trabalho com ela. Nos conhecemos e acabo contando muitas coisas para ela, acho que estava precisando **desabafar**. Minha amiga Sheila havia dito que a simpatia dessa **médica** era fora do comum.

- Doutora Márcia, com o fim do meu **casamento** acabei engordando dez quilos e hoje nenhuma de minhas antigas roupas está servindo; meus **joelhos** doem muito, principalmente quando vou subir as **escadas** de uma das escolas onde sou professora. Meu ex-marido me traiu com uma moça muito mais jovem do que eu e acabei descontando todo o meu **sofrimento** na comida; muita fritura, muito doce. Me ajude a mudar! - acabo desabafando para a jovem Márcia.

- Claro que irei te ajudar, **trabalharemos** juntas para que você possa **conquistar** seu bem-estar, pois é fundamental para uma vida mais saudável. Agora você deve pensar um pouco mais em você mesma. **Estudarei** a melhor forma de mudar sua rotina alimentar, sem que sofra muito com a mudança **radical**. Já adianto que correrá no mínimo 3km (três quilômetros) por semana! Você cumprirá metas de curto e longo prazo para criar uma rotina saudável. - disse Dra. Márcia.

- Que maravilha, realizarei tudo **conforme** você planejar, quero voltar a me sentir uma mulher incrível! - respondo para a doutora.

- Eu também já passei por este **processo.** Meu divórcio foi muito doloroso, passei muitos meses triste e com a cabeça baixa, por isso acabei **emagrecendo** em demasia, o que também é ruim para o nosso organismo. O que me ajudou muito foi ingressar no grupo de corrida de rua e iniciar meus **planejamentos** para participar de competições aqui em nossa cidade. Já fiz excelentes tempos de corrida. - disse Dra. Márcia.

- Nossa, que interessante. Quando ainda era **adolescente** participei de algumas corridas pelo colégio, mas larguei o **esporte** quando entrei na faculdade. Como posso entrar neste grupo? Estou interessada, correrei muito este ano! - respondo toda entusiasmada para a doutora.

Enquanto conversávamos, a pedido da nutricionista, subo na balança e levo um verdadeiro susto: engordei mais 2kg (dois quilos) em uma **semana**! Entretanto, em vez de ficar **reclamando** já começo a pensar positivo, pois gostei muito das dicas que a nutricionista me deu. Conversarei até com meus filhos para que possam me vigiar e anotar toda vez que eu comer **gordura** em excesso. A esta altura estou pensando mil coisas ao mesmo tempo.

- Posso te inserir no grupo de corrida nas **redes sociais** e você começará a acompanhar a turma de iniciantes. Como você está sedentária tem que começar devagar, tudo bem? Será um prazer te ter em nosso grupo, você vai adorar! - disse a Dra. Márcia.

- Ótimo, adorei nossa consulta! Adorei as dicas, trabalharei duro para que tudo dê certo. Vou aguardar suas orientações. - respondo.

Por fim, conversamos mais alguns **detalhes** e me despeço com muita esperança de que tudo dará certo; ainda mais com este grupo de corrida, ficarei mais entusiasmada para correr e ainda conhecerei novas pessoas. Agora estou **solteira**!

Ao entrar no grupo, as pessoas saúdam a minha chegada, logo identifico quem são os **iniciantes** e marco de aparecer no próximo **treino**, que aliás será **próximo** da minha casa. Marcado para daqui a dois dias, fico ansiosa e aviso a todos que irei iniciar meus treinos como corredora. Meus filhos reagem de forma superpositiva e encorajam ainda mais o início dessa nova etapa.

Quando chego ao local marcado sou imediatamente bem **recepcionada** por todos e apresentada para o grupo. Como sou nova, duas pessoas ficam atrás do **pelotão** para irem mais **devagar** comigo e me ajudarem. Acho ótimo, pois ainda não consigo acompanhar o pessoal.

Conversando com as duas pessoas que estão me **acompanhando** fico sabendo que o principal objetivo do grupo é completar uma meia maratona que ocorrerá no final do ano. - Complicado!

Eles explicam que o ritmo de treino deve ir aumentando aos poucos e que a prova da meia maratona pode **ser** concluída com mais facilidade intercalando corrida e caminhada; basta não desistir. De início fiquei bem assustada, mas após passar pela segunda semana de treinos e com o acompanhamento nutricional percebo mudanças no meu corpo e me entusiasmo. Começo então a cogitar a **possibilidade** de participar.

Resolvo conversar com a Andreia, amiga que fiz nos treinos de corrida.

- Oi Andreia, como está? Está confirmado nosso treino de amanhã?

- Sim, Joana. E aí, se animou com a meia maratona? Estou te achando mais energética. Você estará mais animada ainda na semana que vem! - responde Andreia.

- Menina, queria conversar contigo sobre isso. Estou realmente pensando em me inscrever para essa meia maratona, tu achas que tenho como **competir**? Gostaria somente de completar a prova. - digo para Andreia.

- Acredito que tu podes completar a prova, sim. Vejo que estás dedicada aos treinos, participarás assim como eu para finalizar a prova. Podemos andar durante o percurso também, não precisa correr o tempo inteiro. Vamos? - Andreia fala comigo.

- Acho que irei **topar** sim. Responderei com mais certeza no treino de amanhã. Até lá! - respondo para ela.

- Ótimo, até amanhã.

Analisando a situação, percebo que se a meia maratona fosse no **mês que vem** provavelmente eu não terminaria a prova, mas como ainda faltam oito meses, posso sim treinar e conseguir. Peço **conselho** para a minha mãe.

Conto toda a história e ela diz que eu devo **definitivamente** fazer a prova, e que estará lá para torcer por mim. Quando chego ao treino conto a novidade para todos, ficam muito felizes e entro para o time da meia maratona para iniciantes, o grupo Manjubinha.

Os treinos são difíceis, não posso mentir, mas a satisfação é muito boa. Começo a aumentar meus treinos e intensificar os tempos de corrida, essa competição irá confirmar se sou capaz ou não. Detalhe, até aquele momento, após seis meses de treinos, já havia perdido toda a gordura que ganhei com a separação e já estava paquerando um colega do grupo.

Agora já faltava pouco para o grande dia. Sei que ao final da prova terei um grande mérito mesmo não conseguindo completar os 21km (vinte e um quilômetros) **propostos**, pois a minha superação era muito mais psicológica do que competitiva. Meu ex-marido não passava mais pela minha cabeça e me sentia muito feliz, fato este notado por várias pessoas ao meu redor.

Com todo o preparo e treinos completados, o dia da meia maratona chega, e com ele uma ansiedade altíssima. Dra. Márcia, a nutricionista que me ajudou no começo, também estava lá pronta para **corrermos** lado a lado. Com o tempo acabamos fortalecendo nossa amizade e tenho certeza de que ela me ajudará ainda mais no futuro.

Percorridos os 21km, alguns caminhando outros correndo e muitas horas depois da **largada** chego ao final da prova. O sentimento de vitória e conquista são inenarráveis e insubstituíveis. **Recomendo** a todos. Que superação de corpo e alma!

Resumo da história

Após seu divórcio Joana ganha muito peso, o que a leva a procurar ajuda de uma nutricionista. Ao conversarem, surge a ideia de iniciar treinos de corrida para ajudar no processo de emagrecimento e recuperação do estilo de vida saudável. O que Joana não esperava era que esses treinos seriam tão importantes para ela e resultariam na corrida de uma maratona.

Summary of the story

After her divorce, Joana gains a lot of weight, which leads her to seek help from a nutritionist. As they talk, the idea of starting race training arises to help with the process of weight loss and recovery of a healthy lifestyle. What Joana did not expect was that these trainings would be so important to her and would result in a marathon run.

Vocabulary

- **professora de inglês:** English teacher
- **costureira:** seamstress
- **divorciada:** divorced
- **completamente:** completely
- **atrás:** ago
- **vaidade:** vanity
- **maquiagem:** make-up
- **balança:** scale
- **atitude:** attitude
- **nutricionista:** nutritionist
- **emagrecer:** to lose weight
- **marcarei:** schedule (future)
- **consulta:** appointment
- **amanhã:** tomorrow
- **clínica:** clinic
- **nome completo:** full name
- **confirmada:** confirmed
- **até amanhã:** see you tomorrow
- **refrigerante:** soda
- **lanchonete:** snack bar
- **lata:** can
- **proibida:** forbidden
- **animada:** lively
- **simpática:** friendly
- **receptiva:** receptive
- **desabafar:** to unburden
- **médica:** doctor
- **casamento:** marriage
- **joelhos:** knees
- **escadas:** stairs
- **sofrimento:** suffering
- **trabalharemos:** we will work
- **conquistar:** to conquer
- **estudarei:** I will study
- **radical:** radical
- **conforme:** as
- **processo:** process
- **emagrecendo:** losing weight
- **planejamentos:** planning
- **adolescente:** teenager
- **esporte:** sport
- **semana:** week
- **reclamando:** complaining
- **gordura:** fat
- **redes sociais:** social media
- **detalhes:** details
- **solteira:** single
- **iniciante:** beginner

- **treino:** training
- **próximo:** next
- **recepcionada:** welcomed
- **pelotão:** pace group / race squad
- **devagar:** slow
- **acompanhando:** following
- **ser:** to be
- **possibilidade:** possibility
- **realmente:** really
- **competir:** to compete
- **topar:** to accept
- **mês que vem:** next month
- **conselho:** advice
- **definitivamente:** definitely
- **propostos:** proposed
- **corrermos:** run
- **largada:** start
- **recomendo:** recommend

Questions about the story

1. **O que levou Joana a começar a correr?**
   a) Perder peso
   b) Melhorar o condicionamento
   c) Encontrar uma nova profissão
   d) Fazer amigos
2. **Quem aconselhou Joana a iniciar os treinos?**
   a) Seu médico
   b) Sua nutricionista
   c) Sua mãe
   d) Seu ex-marido
3. **Quantos quilômetros Joana percorreu na maratona?**
   a) 21
   b) 32
   c) 14
   d) 25
4. **Qual o nome da nutricionista de Joana?**
   a) Dra. Paula
   b) Dra. Márcia
   c) Dra. Joana
   d) Dra. Vitória
5. **O que contribuiu com o ganho de peso de Joana?**
   a) Uma briga com as amigas
   b) Uma viagem
   c) O término de seu casamento
   d) O nascimento de um filho

Answers

1. A
2. B
3. A
4. B
5. C

CHAPTER FOUR

MAIS QUE PERFEITO (THE PORTUGUESE PLUSPERFECT)

Em época de carroça não se anda sem cavalo – In times of wagon, one does not go without a horse

No **horizonte** da encosta de São Pedro podemos avistar a Vila Rica, bela e estonteante cidadela, a mais rica das redondezas. Lá morara toda a **família real** e seu alto escalão do governo do país de Genova. Havia pastos sempre **verdes** e inúmeros equinos aproveitando-se do bom tempo; **fazendas** cheias de famílias abastecidas e felizes com seus trabalhos; **moradores** que nunca sofreram com **desemprego** ou falta de suprimentos no rigoroso **inverno** da região.

Na vila, as pessoas sempre estavam de **bom humor**, o custo-benefício do lugar valia a pena todo o **esforço** de se trabalhar **arduamente**. Destacara-se a família Rocha que tinha sob seu poder o **comércio** de farinha da região. Logo, dominavam a produção de pães e bolos. Nesta família havia o filho mais novo, Roberto, rapaz **tímido**, com uma **curiosidade** voraz sobre a família real que ali habitava.

- Pai, por favor me conte novamente a história de quando a família real se instaurara em nossa **região**. - perguntou Roberto para seu pai, Eli Rocha.

Eli, por sua vez, era um homem **alto** com seus 1,91m de altura e físico robusto, possuía uma **voz** que chamava muita atenção em qualquer lugar que fosse. Dono do comércio de **farinha** e trigo, sempre fora convidado para grandes **jantares** e comemorações no **palácio**. Sua esposa (Rosa) sempre o acompanhava, mas seus cinco filhos (Roberto, Elma, Juliana, Tati e Paulo) em casa ficavam. Com muito apreço ele sentou-se em frente ao seu filho e iniciou a contagem da **história** da família real pela vigésima vez somente naquele ano.

- A história começara há cerca de cento e vinte cinco anos. O **Rei** Arthur, da família real dos Touros, enquanto passeava de cavalo pelas redondezas da Vila, apaixonou-se pelo horizonte e avistou um local perfeito para a **construção** de sua casa de veraneio. Assim, toda uma estrutura fora montada para realizar o seu **desejo**, um **castelo** jamais visto antes. - disse meu pai.

- Conte mais! Adoro essa história, fico imaginando como o Rei Arthur tivera a amplitude de idealizar sua nova casa. **Pensara** ele na construção para ser a nova a capital do reino ou quisera somente uma nova **casa de veraneio**? - perguntei ao meu pai.

- A construção levara cerca de seis anos para ser **concluída**. Dezenas de homens trabalharam na chamada Oasis de Vila Rica, que possuíra dezenas de quartos, jardins de temporada, aras para os cavalos **premiados** que o Rei mandara trazer da Índia, e é claro o lago dos cisnes, o mais bonito já visto em todos os reinos ao redor... - meu pai continuava a contar a história quando fora **interrompido** pela chegada de minha **irmã** mais velha.

Juliana estava **grávida** de seu primeiro filho, a minha irmã esperara por muito tempo por essa gravidez, até usou diversas **ervas** e tratamentos recomendados pelo médico da vila. Era visível a felicidade em seu rosto.

- Bom dia meus amados! Como têm passado? Planejando algum novo doce para vender na **padaria**? Eu adoraria experimentar os novos doces de mamãe. - disse Juliana.

- Como vai, minha doce menina? E meu neto dentro desta **barriga** enorme, irá nascer quando? Nós estávamos aqui relembrando a história de nossa **querida** família real e sua chegada em Vila Rica. Gostaria de ser juntar a nossa conversa? - meu pai respondeu para ela.

- Os Touros?! Realmente tenho muita admiração por nossa rainha! Amanhã ocorrerá a **distribuição** de novos casacos para os mais necessitados, acho essa iniciativa formidável. Vou me sentar para ouvir o resto da história, mas antes vou buscar uma **maçã**. - disse Juliana.

- Pegue uma para mim também! Estou **faminto**, mas o almoço só ficará pronto daqui a duas horas. - Gritei para que Juliana me ouvisse.

- Está bem, jovem! – ela respondeu

Esperamos até que ela voltasse com as maçãs, e ela trouxera consigo além das frutas alguns biscoitos amanteigados que eram uma verdadeira delícia. Minha mãe era muito **talentosa** e passara todas as suas **receitas** para meu irmão Paulo e minha irmã Elma, ambos muito aplicados e esforçados; por isso, a padaria fazia tanto sucesso.

Minha irmã, meu pai e eu sentamos na varanda, estava muito **quente** dentro da casa e precisávamos nos refrescar. Em seguida minha mãe apareceu com um **suco de limão** muito refrescante e então nós três retornamos nossa atenção ao meu velho e bom pai.

- Bom pessoal, naquela época tudo era muito difícil de **transportar**, assim como os materiais para a construção da casa. Tudo tivera que ser levado com muito cuidado, pois haviam ali mármores caríssimos, madeira nobre e muitos outros elementos. O chefe de obras precisara realizar uma verdadeira força tarefa para conseguir **administrar** todos aqueles movimentos. Ufa, vou tomar um pouco desse suco, está muito quente! - disse meu pai.

- Imaginem as mulheres. Deviam sofrer, naquele tempo as **vestimentas** eram muito conservadoras para qualquer situação. Para uma simples caminhada tinham que colocar várias **camadas** de pano. A rainha, na época, tivera dois empregados exclusivamente para ficar abanando seu **rosto** o dia inteiro, e na época mais fria as camadas só aumentavam, pobres mulheres. - disse minha mãe.

- Ainda bem que não nasci nesta **época**. Meu filho precisará ouvir essas histórias para dar mais valor aos avanços da humanidade. - gesticulou Juliana.

- Tempos difíceis, não é mesmo? Mas sem eles não teríamos **evoluído** tanto! – eu disse de forma pensativa.

Meu pai retoma a história e começa a discursar sobre a **importância** das carroças para aquela época. O rei Arthur, como era um ávido cavaleiro, adorava manter seus cavalos saudáveis e bem tratados, procedimento que fez com que ele tomasse bastante **precaução** com os cavalos que puxavam as carroças. Era proibido maltratar e desfazer dos animais, as punições eram severas.

Tais atitudes são lembradas até os tempos de hoje; os cavalos de Vila Rica são **extremamente** bem cuidados, assim como o **boi** que é designado para puxar a carroça. Quando chegam pessoas de outro reino, o fato de tratarmos os cavalos com tanta nobreza sempre é notado, aliás, as **regras** de bons tratos servem também para quem está de passagem.

- Maltratarás um animal **indefeso** ou que está a te ajudar e estarás também a maltratar a ti mesmo! O Rei Arthur sempre falara esta frase em seus **discursos** motivacionais. Os seus sucessores também mantiveram a tradição, assim como o Rei Carlos que hoje está à frente de nossa família real. - explicou meu pai.

- A atual rainha, Emília, também tem verdadeira adoração por animais, possui vários gatos e **cachorros** no castelo real. - Juliana completa a fala de meu pai.

- Com o passar do tempo e a inauguração da casa de veraneio toda a família real resolvera passar alguns **meses** em seus novos aposentos e divertir-se um pouco. O que era para durar apenas quatro meses está durando até os tempos de hoje. O **clima** em nossa região sempre fora tão agradável que ajudou, na época, a mãe de rei Arthur a melhorar seus problemas de respiração; seus filhos brincavam sem preocupação e conheciam mais a natureza; e as obrigações do reinado eram facilmente despachadas por aqui. Bastava agora que o rei convencesse toda sua corte a mudar a capital para Vila Rica. - continuou Eli.

- Não lembrava dessa parte (eu ri), será que fora muito difícil convencer a todos dessa **mudança**? - perguntei para todos.

Toda a rede de **políticos**, **comerciantes** e **estudiosos** estavam na antiga capital, um lugar sem muito brilho que não possuía um riacho, não tinha mais tantas florestas já que era localizada em uma planície. Pensando nisso, o rei tivera a ideia de levar todas as pessoas mais importantes para Vila Rica, onde pudessem acreditar que existia lugar melhor do que antiga capital.

Uma **comitiva** fora instaurada e muitos vieram conhecer o lugar tão prestigiado pela família real na época. A casa de veraneio conseguira acomodar uma boa parte da comitiva, outros ficaram em cabanas muito bem montadas e apreciadas. Ao final de um mês de convívio com o horizonte mais bonito que o rei Arthur já havia avistado, ocorrera uma votação. A vitória para a mudança da capital fora **maciça**; o encanto do lugar era tamanho que muitos por ali já ficaram.

Iniciara-se o processo de mudança para a nova capital, tudo com muita ajuda de carroças que eram a cada dia mais **aprimoradas** para melhorar a vida dos animais que eram usados no serviço.

Na segunda leva de comerciantes viera o primeiro **parente** de nossa família, o senhor Humberto Rocha que trouxera em sua mala muita força de vontade e inovação. Em suas negociações conseguira trazer os mais diversos produtos e sempre prezava pelo preço **justo.** Rapidamente conquistara fama de bom comerciante. Logo conhecera minha tataravó Joana que era filha de um comerciante de algodão, os dois então construíram o brasão de nossa família e toda nossa tradição.

Meu pai se enche de **orgulho** ao contar essa história, pois meu avô adorava contar também. Nós, os Rocha, somos muito queridos pela vila e pretendo levar isso para toda vida.

Resumo da história

Roberto é um amigável morador de Vila Rica, cidade marcada pela presença de uma família real. Fascinado por história, ele sempre pede a seu pai que conte como tudo evoluiu em sua cidade, o que lhe traz conhecimento sobre sua origem e cultura de onde vive.

Summary of the story

Roberto is a friendly resident of Vila Rica, a city marked by the presence of a royal family. Fascinated by history, he always asks his father to tell how everything evolved in his city, which brings him knowledge about his origin and the culture from where he lives.

Vocabulary

- **horizonte:** horizon
- **família real:** royal family
- **verdes:** green
- **fazendas:** farms
- **moradores:** residents
- **desemprego:** unemployment
- **inverno:** winter
- **bom humor:** good mood
- **esforço:** effort
- **arduamente:** hard
- **comércio:** business
- **tímido:** shy
- **curiosidade:** curiosity
- **região:** region
- **alto:** tall
- **voz:** voice
- **farinha:** flour
- **jantares:** dinners
- **palácio:** palace
- **história:** story
- **Rei:** King
- **construção:** construction
- **desejo:** desire
- **castelo:** castle
- **pensara:** thought
- **casa de veraneio:** summer house
- **concluída:** finished
- **premiados:** awarded
- **interrompidos:** interrupted
- **irmã:** sister
- **grávida:** pregnant
- **ervas:** herbs
- **padaria:** bakery
- **barriga:** belly
- **querida:** dear
- **distribuição:** distribution
- **maçã:** apple
- **faminto:** starving
- **talentosa:** talented
- **receitas:** recipes
- **quente:** hot
- **suco de limão:** lime juice
- **transportar:** to transport
- **administrar:** to administrate
- **vestimentas:** clothing
- **camadas:** layers
- **rosto:** face
- **época:** time
- **evoluído:** evolved
- **importância:** importance
- **precaução:** precaution
- **extremamente:** extremely

- **boi:** ox
- **regras:** rules
- **indefeso:** helpless
- **discursos:** speeches
- **cachorros:** dogs
- **meses:** months
- **clima:** climate
- **mudança:** change
- **políticos:** politicians
- **comerciantes:** retailers
- **estudiosos:** scholars
- **comitiva:** fellowship
- **maciça:** massive
- **aprimoradas:** improved
- **parente:** relative
- **justo:** fair
- **orgulho:** pride

Questions about the story

1. **Que Rei foi responsável pelo início da história de Vila Rica?**

    a) D. João
    b) Rei César
    c) D. Manoel
    d) Rei Arthur

2. **Há quantos anos começa a história contada pelo pai?**

    a) 125
    b) 100
    c) 45
    d) 200

3. **O que foi construído por Rei Arthur após sua chegada?**

    a) Um prédio
    b) Um castelo
    c) Uma taverna
    d) Uma fonte

4. **Qual o sobrenome da família real?**

    a) Touros
    b) Silva
    c) Santos
    d) Arthur

5. **O que a família Rocha tomava durante a história?**

    a) Suco de limão
    b) Cerveja
    c) Refrigerante
    d) Vinho

Answers

1. D
2. A
3. B
4. A
5. A

CHAPTER FIVE

FUTURO DO PRETÉRITO

Eu já previa ter uma nova visão sobre a vida – I already foresaw a new vision about life

Eu sou a gatinha Juju. Tenho seis meses de idade, minha mãe morreu e meus irmãos também. Eu não seria a única da família a **sobreviver** se não tivesse sido **resgata** ainda **recém-nascida** por meus donos, os Jacksons. Sou muito grata a eles por isso.

Minha casa é enorme, tenho muitos lugares para brincar, dormir (muito importante) e ficar bisbilhotando a vida dos meus amigos gatos que moram na casa ao lado. Contarei uma **breve** história de quando cheguei em minha casa. Preparem-se e sejam **fortes**!

Era uma terça-feira e estava caindo uma **chuva** torrencial, quando acordei na caixinha onde ficávamos e me lembrei que estava sozinha, com frio, fome e muito medo de algo ruim acontecer, pois existem pessoas ruins nesse mundo.

Saí perambulando pelas ruas, quase **desmaiando** de fome; quase não, acabaria desmaiando próximo a uma **padaria**. De repente acordei. Estava dentro de um carro sendo levada para algum lugar. Vi que estava no colo de uma mulher com **cabelos loiros** e usando **óculos** de grau vermelhos e com uma roupa muito **fofa** (ela seria minha nova mamãe).

Chegamos em um lugar onde predominava a cor branca e tinha um rapaz vestido com um **jaleco** também branco. Não entendi nada.

Quando dei por mim estava deitada em uma cama muito confortável, com um negócio dentro da minha pata e dele entrava uma espécie de água em meu **corpo.** Achei estranho, mas estava me sentindo muito melhor. Escutei duas pessoas **conversando** e percebi que falavam sobre mim.

- Senhorita Maria, sua gatinha estará bem logo, mas devo te **alertar** que ela está muito **fraca**. Ela deve ter passado muito tempo **abandonada** nas ruas. Seus dentinhos estão frágeis, seu peso está muito abaixo do normal e com a **cirurgia** irá demorar algum tempo para ficar totalmente boa. - disse o moço com jaleco branco para aquela moça loira.

No momento ficaria sem entender. Que cirurgia? O que teria **acontecido** comigo? Foi quando percebi que estava sem a minha patinha traseira e só então começaria a lembrar do que realmente aconteceu naquele dia em que fui resgatada.

Quando estava na rua cambaleando de fome caí no meio da pista e fui atropelada por uma moto. Minha **pata** ficou toda fraturada e sentia tanta dor que acabei desmaiando novamente e acordando já no carro. Cena forte, não é?

- Eu poderia ter morrido naquele dia! Poderia ter tido um **fim** muito pior!

Percebi que estava em uma espécie de **hospital** para animais. Toda hora vinha alguém para checar como eu estava, eu recebia tanto **carinho**... isso nunca tinha acontecido comigo. Minha **comida** chegava na hora certa, não precisava ficar bebendo aquela água barrenta.

Mas voltemos à minha pata perdida. Quando percebi que estava sem ela, entrei em choque, não conseguia acreditar, tentei andar alguns **segundos** e caia com muita facilidade. Os moços que cuidavam de mim sempre tentavam me ajudar a andar, mesmo que fosse pouco. Ali eu ainda tentaria caminhar muitas vezes antes de ir para casa.

Quando ficava sozinha no meu quadradinho pensava em como seria minha vida após sair daquele lugar. Será que conseguiria correr? Teria algum amigo para me ajudar? Comida! Onde eu arrumaria comida com uma pata a menos? Muitas **dúvidas**, muitas dúvidas.

No dia seguinte, fui buscada na **jaula** onde estava e levada para um lugar bem cheiroso. Lá havia outros animais que estavam muito cheirosos também. Fui colocada dentro de um tanque onde começariam a jogar água **morna** em mim pela primeira vez. Foi horrível. Achei que água era feita somente para beber, e eles estavam a jogando em mim.

Reparei que tinha um buraco por onde a água ia embora, ela passava pelo meu corpo e saia dele toda suja de cor marrom. Só assim perceberia que eu estava realmente precisando daquilo. Relaxei e **deixei** a moça fazer todo aquele processo. Ao voltar para minha jaula estava muito cheirosa, muito **confortável**, não queria ir embora nunca!

A moça dos cabelos loiros retornou e veio falar comigo.

- Juju! Seu nome é Juju! Ouviu bem? - disse a moça loira.

Este momento foi incrível, eu tinha um nome agora! Fiquei tão feliz que comecei a fazer uns barulhos estranhos, não conseguia parar, mas a moça estava **adorando**. O moço do jaleco branco apareceu novamente.

- A Juju está pronta para ir embora. Já pode levá-la para casa! Não é ótimo? Vamos à minha sala para repassarmos as **recomendações** de tratamento. - disse o moço.

Comecei a entrar em desespero. Se eu ia embora teria que voltar para as ruas? O que fizera de **errado**? Estava tão bem ali, e logo iria retornar para aquele mundo cruel! Eu partiria novamente para as ruas, que notícia triste.

A moça retornou e colocou uma caixa cheia de furos ao meu lado. Como eu era **filhote** e não tinha muita força ela facilmente conseguiria me colocar ali. Eu diria que estava muito **triste** naquela hora. Achei que tinha feito algo errado, mas meus planos para o futuro incluiriam aquela moça, eu ainda iria fazer muito carinho nela. Já tinha planejado ser muito dócil e ser **companheira**.

Entramos **novamente** naquele carro e andamos por cerca de meia hora. Eu acabaria adormecendo na caixinha e já acordaria em minha nova casa. Naquela altura aquele ainda era um lugar estranho para mim, embora tenha achado muito bonito. Tinha muitas coisas diferentes, tinha até retratos da moça loira ao lado de um rapaz **ruivo**. Gostei. No entanto, tive medo. Quem seria ele? Estava **perdida**.

De repente, levantei-me e logo lembraria que não tinha mais uma de minhas patas, mas já tinha adquirido um certo **equilíbrio** para poder andar. Deveria lembrar sempre de levantar com calma, quando fazia isso apressadamente ficava tonta e caia.

Reparei que tinha algo em meu **pescoço**. O que aquilo fazia em meu pescoço? Não sabia responder, mas logo esqueceria que estava ali e iria **explorar** aquele lugar desconhecido.

Ao andar um pouco senti um forte **cheiro** de algo muito delicioso, comecei a tentar **decifrar** onde estava. Achei uma vasilha cheia de ração! Comi muito, até fiquei com a barriguinha cheia. Resolvi tirar um **cochilo**, e daria aquela volta na casa depois!

Retornei à minha caixinha e lá dormi por algumas horas, estava muito cansada. Eis que **senti** algo me puxando, seria a moça loira? Quando abri os olhos, era o rapaz ruivo! Ele estava falando comigo de um jeito estranho.

- Quem é a gatinha mais bonitinha da casa? A Juju! - disse o ruivo.

Ele fazia um monte de **perguntas** que ele mesmo respondia em seguida. Achei estranho e pensei em sair dali, mas como o carinho que ele fazia em mim **valia a pena** não liguei. A moça loira logo chegaria e me pegaria no colo e continuaria a fazer carinho também.

- Eu cantarei para você, Juju! Cantaria o dia inteiro. A gatinha mais bonita da cidade... - disse a moça loira.

- Ela parece estar gostando do seu colo, está até **ronronando**! Quando vamos apresentá-la ao Lilo? - disse o ruivo.

- Lilo? Quem era Lilo? Seria outro gato? Outro humano para conhecer? Como faria para ser sua **amiga**? Sem uma patinha, ele iria reparar e poderia não gostar. Mas quem será o Lilo? Pensei, pensei e pensei.

Quando olho para o lado de fora da casa vejo quem era o Lilo. Era um **cachorrinho** pequeno todo preto com uma manchinha branca na testa. Ele ficava me olhando e gritando (acho que o nome é **latir**) e ficava abanando o rabo o tempo inteiro.

- Ah, acho que poderíamos levar agora, o que acha? Assim, eles se conheceriam logo e observaríamos o **comportamento** dos dois. - disse a moça loira.

- Acho que é uma boa ideia. Vamos lá! - disse o ruivo.

Quando percebi, ele estava indo em direção àquela **porta** onde o Lilo esperava. Ao abri-la o cachorro entrou numa **rapidez**... Eu teria que ter coragem para encarar aquele afobado!

Ele chegou até mim e começou a me **lamber** toda. Poxa, eu estava tão cheirosa! Agora estou toda babada. Mas resolvo dar uma chance para ele, afinal ele seria meu novo amigo.

Pulei para o chão e tentei andar um pouco e quando olhei para Lilo vi que ele tem as mesmas dificuldades que eu: uma de suas patas traseiras também não estava lá. Eu teria **jurado** que não tinha visto. Nossos donos sorriem muito emocionados.

Caramba! Minha nova casa era **legal**, espaçosa, **divertida**; lá eu teria amigos ao longo da vida, comida na **vasilha**; faria de tudo para que essa família nunca ficasse triste. Ora, mas como ficariam tristes com o Lilo e eu como **animais de estimação**?

Os dias eram muito proveitosos, o Lilo vivia me **chamando** para brincar, íamos até o quintal do vizinho para chamar nossos outros amigos. Levaríamos horas para brincar com todos os animais que moram em nossa rua.

A gata que estaria abandonada na rua, hoje está muito feliz. Eu achava que a deficiência me impediria de **sonhar** e ser feliz; não impede, nem a mim, nem ao Lilo. A vida é uma dádiva e temos que aproveitá-la com **sabedoria.**

Resumo da história

Após sofrer um acidente e passar por tempos difíceis nas ruas, uma gatinha encontra uma nova família, que cuida de seus ferimentos e a leva para seu novo lar. Lá, ela faz seu novo amigo, um cachorrinho simpático que também passou por dificuldades antes de ser acolhido.

Summary of the story

After suffering an accident and going through difficult times on the streets, a kitten meets a new family, who takes care of her injuries and takes her to her new home. There, she makes a new friend, a nice puppy who also went through difficulties before being rescued.

Vocabulary

- **resgatada:** rescued
- **recém-nascida:** newborn
- **sobreviver:** to survive
- **breve:** brief
- **fortes:** strong
- **chuva:** rain
- **desmaiando:** fainting
- **padaria:** bakery
- **cabelos loiros:** blond hair
- **óculos:** glasses
- **fofa:** cute
- **jaleco:** coat
- **corpo:** body
- **conversando:** talking
- **alertar:** to alert
- **fraca:** weak
- **abandonada:** abandoned
- **cirurgia:** surgery
- **acontecido:** happened
- **pata:** paw
- **fim:** end
- **hospital:** hospital
- **carinho:** affection
- **comida:** food
- **segundos:** seconds
- **dúvidas:** doubts
- **jaula:** cage
- **morna:** warm
- **reparei:** noticed
- **deixei:** let
- **confortável:** comfortable
- **adorando:** adoring
- **recomendações:** recommendations
- **errado:** wrong
- **filhote:** puppy
- **triste:** sad
- **companheira:** companion
- **primeira:** first
- **ruivo:** red hair
- **perdida:** lost
- **de repente:** suddenly
- **equilíbrio:** balance
- **pescoço:** neck
- **explorar:** to explore
- **cheiro:** smell
- **decifrar:** to decipher
- **cochilo:** nap
- **senti:** felt
- **perguntas:** questions
- **valia a pena:** was worth it
- **ronronando:** purring
- **amiga:** friend
- **cachorrinho:** puppy
- **latir:** to bark
- **comportamento:** behavior
- **porta:** door

- **rapidez:** speed
- **lamber:** to lick
- **jurado:** sworn
- **emocionados:** excited
- **legal:** cool
- **divertida:** funny
- **vasilha:** bowl
- **animais de estimação:** pets
- **chamando:** calling
- **sonhar:** to dream
- **sabedoria:** wisdom

Questions about the story

1. **Qual o nome da gatinha?**

    a) Juju
    b) Jacksons
    c) Lilo
    d) Ruiva

2. **Por que ela desmaiou antes de ser resgatada?**

    a) Porque estava com fome
    b) Porque sofreu um acidente
    c) Porque sofreu uma queda
    d) Porque tinha sede

3. **Para onde Juju foi levada antes de ir para a casa?**

    a) Um restaurante
    b) Uma escola
    c) Um hospital
    d) Uma casa de banho

4. **Que animal se tornou amigo de Juju?**

    a) Um cachorro
    b) Outro gato
    c) Um pássaro
    d) Um hamster

5. **Quantos humanos viviam com Juju?**

    a) 1
    b) 2
    c) 3
    d) 4

Answers

1. A
2. B
3. C
4. A
5. B

CHAPTER SIX

PARTICIPLE AND ABUNDANT VERBS

O estagiário e as notícias –
The trainee and the news

Meu nome é Vanessa e sou **jornalista**, redatora chefe no maior jornal local. Trabalho com **atualidades** e vivo em função dos acontecimentos buscando notícias, **manchetes** e revisando matérias para lançar. Você já imaginou como o mundo seria se não tivéssemos os **meios de comunicação** que temos hoje? Como teríamos acesso às informações sobre o mundo? Sempre fico pensando nisso.

Fico me perguntando como seria a vida em uma realidade **paralela**, por exemplo. E ao lidar com **notícias**, às vezes também penso o que teria feito pessoas cometerem **crimes** ou realizar boas ações; se **catástrofes** poderiam ser evitadas ou se simplesmente estamos esperando as coisas acontecerem. Minha **avó** sempre dizia que se você não corre atrás dos seus sonhos, alguém vai correr. E sabe o que mais? Você provavelmente estará trabalhando para ajudar alguém a realizar os sonhos dele, enquanto os seus serão esquecidos.

Bem, a verdade é que muita gente apenas **sobrevive**, não busca ser protagonista da própria vida e acaba não pensando o que poderia fazer de diferente para mudar uma realidade. **Realidade**. Essa palavra é muito forte também nos meios de comunicação e no mundo das notícias. Um fato já é algo real, não sejamos redundantes. Mas é no mundo da **ficção** que nossa imaginação transborda e nos deixa mais criativos.

Era o que fazia o **estagiário** do jornal onde eu trabalhava, que era meu assistente para **redigir** matérias e cuidar de tudo mais que eu precisasse. João era um cara animadíssimo, muito entusiasmado e atualizado em todos os assuntos, sabia de tudo o que estava acontecendo, acompanhava as manchetes como **ninguém**! Certa vez, ele chegou à redação eufórico:

- Vanessinha!!! Querida, você viu o que rolou ontem? – disse João.

- Ah, foram tantas coisas, seja mais específico. – eu disse.

- **Finalmente** a nossa matéria foi aceita. – disse João.

- Como assim? Qual **matéria**? – eu disse, sem nem mesmo me lembrar.

- Para a revista de entretenimento do jornal, não lembra? Fizemos um texto sobre Belém, que foi eleita *Cidade Criativa da Gastronomia* pela Unesco. A capital do Pará virou referência mundial em **gastronomia**, pois está entre as 116 cidades criativas em todo o mundo.

- Ah, é verdade! Lembrei desse artigo, ficou ótimo! Graças a você, João! Sem seu empenho, nós não conseguiríamos! – eu disse.

João ficava **lisonjeado**, mas não gostava de demonstrar. Ele estava no caminho certo para se tornar um ótimo jornalista, eu não tinha dúvidas disso. Ele tinha vontade de **ascender** na vida, trabalhava muito e sempre estava um passo à frente dos demais. Mas como nem tudo é perfeito João me enlouquecia um pouco, pois era **ansioso** e às vezes falava muito. Era preciso muita atenção para acompanhar o **raciocínio** dele e não me perder no que ele estava falando:

- Vanessa, já está tudo resolvido, os contatos já foram feitos e precisamos mandar um jornalista para cobrir o evento de **lançamento** dos shows da cantora em Las Vegas! Quem vai ser?

- O Mário. Ele já está sabendo, mas lhe envie um e-mail para lembrá-lo, por favor. – disse.

- O Mário? Hum. – disse João com ar de **ciúmes**. E continuou:

- Vanessa, as reservas foram enviadas pelo funcionário da empresa de **viagens** para o e-mail do Mário. Nossa, eu teria morrido de surpresa se eu trabalhasse aqui e fosse escolhido para ir pra Las Vegas. Você me escolheria?

- Uhum – murmurei sem prestar atenção.

- Vanessa, você viu que uma moça aqui da nossa cidade ganhou na **Loteria**? Não acredito que ela tenha ganhado toda essa fortuna no jogo. Se fosse você, o que faria se ganhasse 32 milhões de reais? - indagou João.

Sim. Ele falava sem parar. Minha sorte é que eu só escutava: - Blá, blá, blá.

- **CHEFE**! – Ele fala mais alto.

- Hun? – eu murmuro.

- Eu perguntei o que você faria se ganhasse tanto dinheiro na loteria. – disse João.

- Eu? Ah, faria **doações** para creches, lar dos velhinhos, hospitais de câncer infantil, faria eventos beneficentes. Acho que é muito dinheiro para uma pessoa apenas, é possível fazer o bem para muita gente com essa quantia toda. – disse.

- Nossa, como você é **generosa**! – disse João. – Eu, imaginando aqui, em um primeiro momento só pensei em mim mesmo. Pensei em viajar, conhecer o mundo... eu nunca saí do Brasil. Eu levaria você, Vanessa! A gente rodaria o mundo, conheceríamos as **sedes** dos principais jornais, os veículos de informação mais importantes do mundo, seria um sonho! Depois faríamos doações, é claro. Eu teria muito tempo para planejar tudo e aproveitar ao mesmo tempo.

- Não se ache **egoísta**, você só quer conhecer o mundo, isso é bem plausível. Eu sei que cedo ou tarde você faria doações também, já que vem de uma origem **humilde**, assim como eu. É dito que os mais humildes são os que mais ajudam os outros, sabia? – eu disse.

- É, eu imagino. – disse João.

- Ah, imaginar é com você mesmo! Vive no mundo da lua! Você pelo menos joga na loteria? Ou só gosta de imaginar mesmo?

- Vou jogar, Vanessa... vou jogar. – disse ele ficando desanimado.

- Agora enquanto você não fica rico, cadê a matéria que a redatora deixou pronta e revisada ontem? – eu perguntei.

- Ah, pois é, quando ela foi embora, você ainda não tinha voltado da reunião, e a **secretária** saiu sem ter acendido as luzes do escritório. Como estavam todas apagadas, a moça pensou que não havia ninguém e foi embora. – ele disse.

- Sim, e cadê ela agora? – indaguei.

- Não vai vir hoje, passou mal e foi ao hospital, parece que vai ser **internada**. Por sorte ela já tinha terminado o texto, então vou pegar uma cópia no computador dela. – respondeu João.

- Sim, faça isso rapidamente. E depois vá ao hospital ver como ela está e se precisa de algo, pegue, leve essas **flores** que estão aqui nesse jarro. – eu disse.

- Eu? Como assim? E essas flores estão murchas! Acho que não teriam murchado tão depressa se você as tivesse posto em um lugar mais arejado. – ele diz enquanto verifica as flores.

- É, João! Você... Isabela mora **sozinha** aqui em São Paulo, a família dela é toda do Amazonas. Vai logo, não precisa voltar hoje. – eu disse – mantenha-me informada.

- É mesmo? Humm. Tudo bem. Sabia que no Brasil, três línguas indígenas são aceitas como línguas oficiais desde 2002? No munícipio de São Gabriel da Cachoeira no Amazonas são consideradas como línguas oficiais, além do português, o Nheengatu, Baniwa e Tukano. – tagarelou João.

- Eu vou te dar mais cinco minutos para sair desse prédio. Vá! – ordenei.

- Não está mais aqui quem falou. Fui! – disse João ao sair correndo.

O que João não sabia é que faríamos uma festa de aniversário surpresa para ele na redação. Claro que eu estava preocupada com a Isabela, mas também aproveitei para tirar o João do local de trabalho para **combinarmos** tudo.

Feito isso, combinamos com todos os colegas uma **festa** para o dia seguinte. O **aniversário** de João era nesta semana, então resolvemos adiantar a data, pois ele era terrível, sempre descobria tudo, pois ficava de orelha em pé e no ano passado não conseguimos fazer algo **surpresa**; ele percebeu toda a nossa movimentação.

No dia seguinte, a secretária Cristina chegou bem cedo. Ela sabia que a encomenda do bolo, salgados e **refrigerantes** chegaria às 15h (quinze horas), então buscaria o "café" nesse momento. Eu ficaria **responsável** de arrumar alguma tarefa para o João fazer em outro setor do nosso Jornal, em que ele demorasse bastante para ir e voltar.

O dia passou normalmente e após retornamos do **almoço**, entro na sala e pisco para Cristina. Dou boa tarde a todos na redação e como sempre, estamos trabalhando muito, então falo bem alto para todos trabalharem rapidamente, deixarem as demandas prontas porque teremos uma reunião às 16h nesse setor.

- João, cadê as matérias do caderno de entretenimento desta semana? Você ficou de organizar tudo e eu não quero atrasos! – eu falo eufórica (e encenando um pouco).

- Chefe, já está tudo sob controle, não se preocupe com isso, já está tudo impresso. – ele diz me tranquilizando.

- Então me conta, como foi lá no hospital ontem? Como está a Isabela? – eu perguntei.

- Nossa, ontem não foi o meu dia, tive que pegar dois ônibus para chegar até lá, porque peguei o **ônibus** errado.

- E por que não foi de Uber? Era só ter me falado.

- Eu sou estagiário, estou acostumado a andar de **transporte público**, além de ser mais barato. O problema é que o hospital era **longe**, nunca tinha ido lá. Mas depois acertei. Assim que cheguei ao hospital vi uma mãe gritando porque seu filho foi morto em um **assalto**. Foi horrível. Esses marginais deveriam ser presos em flagrante.

- João, de notícia ruim já basta as que vemos aqui no jornal. E como está Isabela? – cortei a fala de João.

- Está bem, chefe, na medida do possível. Ela passou mal, estava com cálculo renal, vai fazer a cirurgia para a retirada, é mais simples, a **recuperação** é rápida. Agora, difícil vai ser o meu **joelho** parar de doer, pois escorreguei no quarto em que ela estava internada. A moça da limpeza disse que havia enxugado o chão, mas não ficou bem enxuto porque o dia estava muito úmido. À propósito, entreguei as flores. Disse que estamos esperando por ela e desejei boa recuperação. – falou sem respirar João.

- Ah, que bom que ela já está assistida. E você, cuidado onde pisa! Cuidado com esse joelho. Ah, aproveita que está aí em pé e vá levar esses documentos lá no setor de contabilidade. – eu disse.

- Eu digo que estou com o joelho ruim e você já me manda trabalhar mais? Ok, ok. Lá na **contabilidade**??? Vou demorar quase meia hora. – resmungou João.

- Vai logo, João! – E não demora muito pois teremos reunião em 15 minutos! – ordenei.

Assim que ele saiu, Cristina trouxe a encomenda de aniversário, os outros colegas trouxeram **balões**, chapeuzinhos, apitos e as letras para pendurar na parede que diziam: Parabéns, João!

Quando João voltou, todo agoniado falando que correu para não perder a reunião, cantamos os parabéns com muita empolgação. Vocês precisavam ver a cara dele, foi pego de surpresa! Ficou pálido, morreu de rir e depois **chorou**. Disse que nunca tinha tido uma festa de aniversário surpresa e que não estava esperando por isso.

Todos ficaram muito felizes e logo o **bolo** foi partido por João. Ele disse que o primeiro pedaço iria para Cristina, pois todos éramos muitos especiais, mas ela era a primeira a chegar e praticamente a última a ir embora e ainda nos fazia um café maravilhoso, nos deixando animados para o trabalho. Era verdade.

- João, mudando de assunto, chegou um envelope aqui para você. – eu disse.

- O que é, chefe? Não vai dizer que é mais trabalho?! Ainda nem terminei de comer. – ele disse morrendo de rir.

- Abre logo, engraçadinho! – pedi que o fizesse.

João abriu o envelope e mal podia acreditar. Chorou mais uma vez, de emoção, é claro. Como ele estava prestes a se formar, a empresa decidiu pedir sua contratação assim que estivesse com o **diploma**. João não ganhou na loteria, mas ganhou uma proposta de emprego em nosso jornal. Certamente para ele foi um grande prêmio.

Resumo da história

João é um estagiário muito dedicado, e que às vezes fala demais. Após tagarelar sobre diversos assuntos, sua chefe o manda fazer uma visita a uma colega de trabalho que está internada, e aproveita para preparar para ele uma festa surpresa. Será que João vai descobrir os planos de Vanessa?

Summary of the story

João is a very dedicated trainee, and sometimes he talks too much. After chattering on various subjects, his boss orders him to visit a co-worker who is hospitalized and takes the opportunity to prepare a surprise party for him. Is João going to discover Vanessa's plan?

Vocabulary

- **jornalista:** journalist
- **atualidades:** news
- **manchetes:** headlines
- **meios de comunicação:** means of communication
- **paralela:** parallel
- **notícias:** news
- **crimes:** crimes
- **catástrofes:** catastrophes
- **avó:** grandmother
- **sobrevive:** survive
- **realidade:** reality
- **ficção:** fiction
- **estagiário:** intern
- **redigir:** to write
- **ninguém:** no one
- **finalmente:** finally
- **matéria:** article
- **gastronomia:** gastronomy
- **lisonjeado:** flattered
- **ascender:** to grow
- **ansioso:** anxious
- **raciocínio:** reasoning
- **lançamento:** launch
- **ciúmes:** jealousy
- **viagens:** trips
- **loteria:** lottery
- **chefe:** boss
- **doações:** donations
- **generosa:** generous
- **sedes:** headquarters
- **egoísta:** selfish
- **humilde:** humble
- **secretária:** secretary
- **internada:** hospitalized
- **flores:** flowers
- **sozinha:** alone
- **combinarmos:** arrange
- **festa:** party
- **aniversário:** birthday
- **surpresa:** surprise
- **refrigerantes:** sodas
- **responsável:** in charge
- **almoço:** lunch
- **ônibus:** bus
- **transporte público:** public transportation
- **longe:** far
- **assalto:** robbery
- **recuperação:** recovery
- **joelho:** knee
- **contabilidade:** accounting
- **balões:** balloons
- **chorou:** cried
- **bolo:** cake
- **diploma:** university Degree

Questions about the story

1. Qual a profissão de Vanessa?

a) Jornalista
b) Médica
c) Escritora
d) Motorista

2. Qual característica melhor descreve João?

a) Introvertido
b) Animado
c) Triste
d) Nervoso

3. Por que Vanessa queria João fora do escritório?

a) Porque ele atrapalhava o trabalho
b) Porque o local estava muito cheio
c) Porque era seu aniversário
d) Porque Vanessa queria ficar sozinha

4. Qual foi a desculpa usada por Vanessa para afastar João do escritório?

a) Visitar uma colega no hospital
b) Visitar um cliente
c) Tirar um dia de folga
d) Ir ao banco

5. Qual foi a reação de João com a surpresa?

a) Ele chorou de emoção
b) Ele chorou de tristeza
c) Ele ficou bravo
d) Ele não se surpreendeu

Answers

1. A
2. B
3. C
4. A
5. A

CHAPTER SEVEN

PASSIVE

Brasil, um país diverso – Brasil, a diverse country

Meu nome é Fausto e esta **empresa** de turismo aqui no Brasil é **gerenciada** por mim. Sei mais do que ninguém que a diversidade cultural atrai **turistas** para as cinco **regiões** brasileiras. As expressões artísticas e culturais convidam visitantes a desfrutar de um dos cenários mais ricos e multifacetados do mundo. Por isso, estou sempre buscando meios de **divulgar** os costumes e as paisagens naturais maravilhosas de cada **estado** brasileiro.

Muitas **propagandas** que faço em minha **agência de turismo** servem não somente para turistas **estrangeiros**, mas para os próprios brasileiros que não conhecem tão bem o **território** nacional, afinal, trata-se de um país com dimensões continentais. Na Europa, por exemplo, você faz um voo curto e já está em outro país; no Brasil, você no máximo cruza a fronteira para outro estado.

Gosto muito do meu país e sou **defensor** das nossas músicas, danças, festas populares, **culinária** e **artesanato**. Diversas manifestações artísticas fazem do nosso Brasil um dos destinos turísticos mais procurados por quem quer conhecer de perto a **imensa** diversidade cultural que temos. São muitos os adeptos das nossas tradições e costumes, pois estes circulam pelos quatro cantos do país, ultrapassando muitas vezes até mesmo nossas **fronteiras** e **angariando** admiradores, visitantes que se **encantam** com a potencialidade da cultura brasileira. As nossas cinco regiões são **riquíssimas** em manifestações artístico-culturais e vou mostrar o porquê.

A região Nordeste do Brasil é muito famosa por sua natureza exuberante e também possui uma cultura **expressiva**. Todos os anos, no Carnaval, milhares de carnavalescos do mundo inteiro são atraídos para o Nordeste, pois Salvador, a capital baiana, conhecida pelo **ritmo** do axé, tem um dos carnavais mais famosos do país. Recife, a capital de Pernambuco, é palco para os blocos de rua **tradicionais** e o ritmo frevo, dançado com roupas de pierrô e um **guarda-chuva** colorido, atraindo os foliões para pular o carnaval.

Já no mês de junho, as festas em homenagem a São João tomam conta da região Nordeste. São festas muito tradicionais, e por acontecerem nesse mês são chamadas de festas juninas. Todos dançam ao som do Forró, um ritmo bem nordestino, típico da região. Nessa época o turista fica dividido, precisando escolher entre Caruaru, no Pernambuco ou Campina Grande, na Paraíba. Os dois destinos são fantásticos, **cheios** da dança, quadrilhas, gastronomia local e artesanato.

O Nordeste também é conhecido pela influência da **cultura africana**, seja na música (Cavalhada, Moçambique, Maracatu, Congada e etc.), na religião (Candomblé) e na gastronomia (caruru, vatapá, canjica, mungunzá, acarajé, quindim e pamonha), isso sem falar na influência linguística.

Agora, mais para o centro do país, na região Centro-Oeste, Brasília é a **principal** atração turística, integrando o Distrito Federal. A Unesco (Organização das Nações Unidas para a Educação, Ciência e Cultura) reconheceu Brasília como Patrimônio Cultural da Humanidade.

A capital federal é o centro das **decisões** políticas no País. Planejada por Lúcio Costa e Oscar Niemeyer, possui muitas obras de **destaque** internacional como, por exemplo, o Palácio da Alvorada, o Congresso Nacional, a Catedral de Brasília, a Esplanada dos Ministérios e o Palácio do Planalto.

No estado do Goiás, o destaque vai para Pirenópolis, local de **tranquilidade**, histórico e também de festas culturais, como a Festa do Divino. Possui **cachoeiras, fazendas** e muito artesanato. Em "Piri", apelido carinhoso dado à cidade, o contato com a natureza é intenso e o charme de cidade de interior convida os visitantes a estarem em paz.

Se você gosta de aventura, **acampar**, cachoeiras, estar em contato com a natureza, o bioma do cerrado e suas belezas, um ótimo local para conhecer é a Chapada dos Veadeiros, que fica dentro do Parque Nacional.

Mas se você ainda quer saber de Carnaval, a região Sudeste também pode ser uma opção. Isso porque todos os anos, durante essa época, **milhares** de pessoas vão para essa região para acompanhar os lindíssimos **desfiles** das escolas de samba no Sambódromo do Rio de Janeiro, na famosa Marquês de Sapucaí.

Por outro lado, se você prefere cidades históricas pode continuar no estado do Rio porque há anualmente a Feira Literária Internacional de Paraty, integrante do circuito dos festivais internacionais de literatura. É uma cidade histórica **charmosa**, a aproximadamente 200 quilômetros da capital do Rio. O único detalhe aqui é que a entrada de veículos é **proibida**, o turista precisará visitar a cidade a pé.

Na região Sudeste também tem a festa do Peão de Barretos, feita no interior de São Paulo, que acontece no mês de agosto, durando aproximadamente dez dias. O ritmo musical tocado é o sertanejo, embalando os rodeios na arena, que também foi projetada pelo arquiteto Oscar Niemeyer, tendo capacidade para aproximadamente 30 mil pessoas.

Se você gosta de **roteiros** arquitetônicos e históricos, precisa conhecer a região central de Minas Gerais, onde ficam **guardadas** algumas das igrejas mais **lindas** do país. Essas igrejas localizadas em Ouro Preto como, por exemplo, a Igreja de Francisco de Assis, foram **construídas** ainda no período colonial. Estas cidades são como museus a **céu aberto**, cheias de detalhes históricos por todos os lados.

Os visitantes podem passear pelas **agradáveis** ruas de pedra sabão em Ouro Preto e conhecer a feira artesanal que fica ao lado da casa de Tomás Antônio Gonzaga e também a Secretaria Municipal de Turismo e Cultura.

O caminho nomeado de Estrada Real é composto por cidades históricas como Congonhas, Tiradentes, Mariana, Sabará e São João Del-Rei. É impossível não perceber o estilo da arte **barroca** marcada pelo bucolismo de um Brasil colônia.

Se o visitante gostar de festas populares e **lendas**, é a região Norte que ele precisa conhecer. Anualmente, milhares de turistas de todos os lugares do Brasil e do mundo vão ao Amazonas para **festejar** em um dos principais eventos de representação do folclore nacional que acontece em junho, o Festival Folclórico de Parintins, conhecida também como a Festa do Boi Bumbá. Essa festa costuma durar três dias e conta uma lenda, uma história de um boi, sua morte e ressureição, além de lendas sobre a rotina dos nativos dali, com muitas danças e toadas de influência indígena.

Se o foco da viagem for o turismo religioso, há também a procissão católica do Círio de Nazaré, que acontece em Belém do Pará. Essa é uma cerimônia que o turista não pode perder, feita para a Santa e **ocorre** sempre em outubro. Muitos fiéis fazem a **caminhada** pelas ruas para homenagear Nossa Senhora de Nazaré.

A região Norte também é conhecida por sua culinária exótica de

raízes indígenas. A base da culinária dessa região são a mandioca, os peixes tanto de água salgada como de água **doce** e muitas frutas exóticas.

Uma região que possui influência marcante da cultura europeia no Brasil é a região Sul. Ao longo da história do país os traços das tradições de imigrantes **alemães**, italianos, espanhóis e portugueses permanecem nesta região. São muitas festas com muita **cerveja**, chimarrão e **vinho**. Destacam-se a Festa da **Uva**, em Caxias do Sul, no Rio Grande do Sul e a Oktoberfest, em Blumenau, Santa Catarina.

A Festa da Uva teve sua tradição iniciada em 1931, em Caxias do Sul, com uma pequena **exposição** de uvas dos produtores coloniais e **atualmente** conta com milhares de visitantes entre fevereiro e março.

Já a Oktoberfest é realizada há mais de vinte anos, todo mês de outubro, com geralmente 500 mil visitantes, contribuindo economicamente para Blumenau, deixando **lotados** os hotéis, bares e outros espaços da cidade.

Sempre que estiver interessado em fazer uma viagem pelo Brasil, mas estiver em dúvida se valerá a pena e se será um lugar interessante, faça uma **pesquisa** sobre o local, os pontos positivos e negativos desse lugar e escolha uma região com base nos seus objetivos de viagem: se é para **descansar** ou se cansar. Vai por mim, esse país vale a pena conhecer.

Resumo da história

Fausto é gerente de uma agência de viagens e adora o que faz! Em seu trabalho, ele aconselha as pessoas a como decidir sobre a melhor viagem para cada perfil. Ele conta sobre as tradicionais festas de cada região do Brasil, país que, em sua opinião, vale muito a pena conhecer, e mostra como cada pedaço dessa enorme nação conta uma história completamente diferente e pode ser apreciada pelos mais diversos públicos.

Summary of the story

Fausto is a travel agency manager and loves what he does! At his work, he advises people on how to decide the best trip for each profile. He talks about the traditional festivals of each region of Brazil, a country he thinks is worth knowing, and shows how each piece of this enormous nation tells a completely different story and can be appreciated by the most diverse publics.

Vocabulary

- **empresa:** company
- **gerenciada:** managed
- **turistas:** tourists
- **regiões:** regions
- **divulgar:** to publicize
- **estado:** state
- **propaganda:** advertisement
- **agência de turismo:** tourism agency
- **estrangeiros:** foreigners
- **território:** territory
- **defensor:** defender
- **culinária:** cuisine
- **artesanato:** handcraft
- **imensa:** huge
- **fronteiras:** frontiers
- **angariando:** raising
- **encantam:** enchant
- **riquíssimas:** very rich
- **expressiva:** significant
- **ritmo:** rythm
- **tradicionais:** traditional
- **guarda-chuva:** umbrella
- **cheios:** full
- **cultura africana:** African culture
- **principal:** main
- **decisões:** decisions
- **destaque:** highlight
- **tranquilidade:** tranquility
- **cachoeiras:** waterfalls
- **fazendas:** farms
- **acampar:** camping
- **milhares:** thousands
- **desfiles:** parades
- **charmosa:** charming
- **proibida:** forbidden
- **roteiros:** routes
- **guardadas:** saved
- **lindas:** beautiful
- **construídas:** built
- **céu aberto:** outdoors
- **agradáveis:** pleasant
- **barroca:** baroque
- **lendas:** legends
- **festejar:** to celebrate
- **ocorre:** happens
- **caminhada:** walk
- **raízes:** roots
- **doce:** sweet
- **alemãs:** German
- **cerveja:** beer
- **vinho:** wine
- **uva:** grape
- **exposição:** expo

- **atualmente:** currently
- **lotados:** crowded
- **pesquisa:** survey
- **descansar:** to rest

Questions about the story

1. **Qual evento marca a região Nordeste?**
    a) Natal
    b) Carnaval
    c) Boi Bumbá
    d) São João
2. **Onde ocorre a festa de Parintins?**
    a) Amazonas
    b) Bahia
    c) Minas Gerais
    d) Rio Grande do Sul
3. **Que cidade foi considerada Patrimônio Cultural pela ONU?**
    a) Goiânia
    b) Manaus
    c) São Paulo
    d) Brasília
4. **Quais as atrações da Chapada dos Veadeiros?**
    a) Esportes de aventura
    b) Compras
    c) Igrejas e edifícios históricos
    d) Aventura, acampamento, cachoeiras
5. **Qual região é ideal para o turismo religioso?**
    a) Norte
    b) Sul
    c) Sudeste
    d) Centro-Oeste

Answers

1. B
2. A
3. D
4. D
5. A

CHAPTER EIGHT

VOCABULARY AND EXPRESSIONS

Na saúde e na doença – In sickness and in health

Marina é uma professora de **física** que acabou de passar em um **concurso** do colégio militar da **aeronáutica** brasileira. Certamente será uma professora muito dedicada, **respeitada** por seus alunos e colegas de trabalho.

Marina já prepara as aulas que dará na aeronáutica, ensinar física é com ela mesmo! Mostrará aos alunos formas mais fáceis de visualizar a **abstração** que essa **disciplina** exige e tentará fazer com que eles gostem dessa **matéria** que tanto encanta Marina. Dessa forma, ela cumprirá com o **dever** de melhorar o ensino no país.

A matéria que Marina mais gosta de ensinar é aerodinâmica aplicada à **aviação**, pois fez mestrado nessa área. Ela ainda é doutora em **mecânica** aplicada à aviação e **ministrará** disciplinas também nessa área que é muito importante no currículo dos estudantes e para a segurança aérea.

Marina sempre foi muito **organizada** e **perfeccionista** em sua vida e trabalho. Não seria diferente dessa vez. Certamente ela deixará tudo organizado e terá controle sobre seus planos e sonhos, assim como ela gosta que seja.

Marina namora Raí, um dentista renomado e que também é **apaixonado** pelo que faz e por ela. Raí a pedirá em casamento em breve, está apenas esperando Marina se adaptar ao novo trabalho.

A melhor amiga de Marina é Adriana, elas se **formaram** juntas no ensino médio e continuaram amigas desde então. Adriana liga para Marina, chamando-a para almoçar daqui a três dias. Ela já convida com **antecedência**, pois sabe que Marina gosta de se programar e geralmente não aceita convites em cima da hora e provavelmente estará com a **agenda** da semana cheia. Marina aceita o convite e na quinta-feira próxima ambas se encontram:

- Amiga, **quanto tempo**!

- É verdade, como você está?

- Ah, na mesma correria de sempre, agora estou dando aulas em um novo **emprego**.

- Que coisa boa, espero que você goste.

- É, já estou adorando.

- E o namoro, como está? Quando Raí vai te pedir em casamento?

- Ah, estamos bem, tudo tranquilo. Não sei, acho que ainda vai **demorar um pouco**.

- Que **besteira**, vocês estão bem, com bons empregos, a vida ajeitada, por que vão esperar mais? Será que ele não está te enrolando? Raí é muito **orgulhoso**, ele nunca dá o braço a torcer.

Adriana está com dor de cotovelo. Na verdade, ela queria ter um namorado tão bonito quanto o da amiga. Mas Marina já estava com a resposta na ponta da língua:

- Eu não sei, não penso muito nisso, na verdade, eu gosto assim, consigo me programar mais e fazer as minhas coisas do jeito que gosto.

- Marina, todo mundo tem medo da vida a dois, a não ser que você queira ficar **sozinha** pra sempre, esse momento vai ter que chegar.

- É, eu sei. Só não quero pensar nisso agora. Mudando de **assunto**, como está sua mãe?

- Ah, está bem. Você sabe, ela fala pelos cotovelos. Quando ela começa, não para mais, fala até sozinha. Ela continua colocando o dedo onde não é chamada, já falei para ela deixar eu resolver meus problemas sozinha.

- Tenha **paciência** com ela, Adriana!

- Eu tenho até demais, amiga.

- E na loja? Como andam as vendas?

- Está indo muito bem, **Graças à Deus**! Mas essa semana aconteceu uma coisa chata: meu funcionário me desrespeitou e por isso eu o mandei para o olho da rua. Você ficaria de cabelo em pé se ouvisse as barbaridades que ele me disse.

- Que horror. Você fez das tripas coração para ajudar aquele homem. Tem gente que não dá valor ao emprego, não é verdade?

- Pois é, não tenho **estômago** para isso. Fiquei exausta com essa situação e não preguei os olhos durante dois dias.

- Fica tranquila. Você vai arrumar outro **funcionário**, uma pessoa boa e responsável.

As duas continuam conversando e após o almoço fazem compras rápidas juntas, as roupas nesse shopping custam os olhos da cara. Marina teve que escolher uma **bolsa** que não chegava aos pés de outra, mas era mais barata.

Adriana pede que Marina a acompanhe numa **cartomante**. Marina recusa, diz que não acredita nessas coisas. Adriana insiste, diz que sempre quis ir, mas não queria ir sozinha. Marina claramente não quer ir, mas fica com **pena** da amiga e vai. A cartomante faz uma previsão radical na vida de Marina, que não acredita.

Na semana seguinte Marina recebe a notícia de mudança de turmas em seu trabalho, ou seja, não vai mais **lecionar** as disciplinas de **outrora** e terá que preparar outras aulas para novas disciplinas, as quais ela não gosta nem um pouco de ensinar.

Marina estava **preocupada**. Como faria com que os alunos gostassem dessa disciplina se nem mesmo ela gostava? Não tinha se **especializado** nessa área, teria que se **desdobrar** para dar conta de tudo.

Para completar, o **dono do apartamento** que Marina alugava pediu que ela saísse, pois precisaria vender o imóvel. Marina se ofereceu para comprar, mas o dono recusou dizendo que já tinha um outro **comprador** e precisava vender com urgência. Ou seja, Marina precisaria procurar outro lugar para morar e fazer sua mudança em pouco mais de um mês.

Além disso, fora surpreendida com um pedido de casamento durante um jantar com Raí e disse que sim, mas queria ter dito "vamos esperar mais um pouco?"

Raí disse que este seria o momento perfeito, que ela poderia mudar logo para o apartamento dele e não precisaria encontrar outro local para morar. Marina não gostou da ideia, mas concordou.

Em sua relutância para encarar as mudanças que estavam acontecendo, Marina passou mal um dia no trabalho e foi parar no hospital. O diagnóstico? **Estafa**, início de **depressão**.

Ela não podia acreditar. Como? O que aconteceu para que chegasse a esse ponto? O que fazer agora? Ela nunca tinha passado por nada parecido, já morava longe da família há tempos; resolvia tudo sozinha, dava conta do recado.

Para piorar a situação, após um tempo, Raí achou que Marina estava inventando essa doença para não dar um passo a diante no **relacionamento** dos dois, mesmo após ela ter concordado em morar com ele. Não poderia ser diferente, ele era muito exigente e queria alguém **saudável** ao seu lado. Disse a Marina que era melhor ela procurar um apartamento para ela.

Marina ligou para sua melhor amiga, Adriana. Pediu para morar com ela e sua mãe por um tempo, até que se sentisse melhor para voltar a morar sozinha. Adriana prontamente a recebeu e concordou que Raí foi muito **inescrupuloso** ao ter feito tudo isso, mas tratou logo de mostrar para a amiga o quanto algumas **mudanças** podem nos fazer bem.

Em uma consulta com sua psicóloga, Marina foi descobrindo mais sobre esta doença e como lidar com ela. A **psicóloga** disse que a depressão era o mal do século, em uma **sociedade** que tanto nos cobra e no cotidiano estressante que muitos enfrentam. Essa palavra passou a fazer parte do dia a dia das mulheres e se tornou muito comum nos tempos atuais.

A psicóloga explicou que quem sofre desse transtorno pode não saber o que é, mas dos sintomas não se esquece, mesmo com o passar do tempo e controle da doença, que faz sua vítima ver sempre o lado **negativo** das situações, mesmo que conheça a realidade e faz com que perca totalmente o interesse pela vida.

A depressão ou também transtorno depressivo, é uma doença psíquica que afeta o **sistema nervoso central**, alterando o humor e a maneira da pessoa lidar com sentimentos diversos relativos à afetividade.

Grande parte das vítimas são mulheres que, perante as pressões sociais do mundo modernizado, a **competitividade** e conciliação da vida pessoal e profissional, acabam ficando mais expostas a doenças. Muitos são os fatores que podem influenciar para que a depressão seja desenvolvida e geralmente estão ligados a fatores genéticos, hereditários, ambientais ou psicológicos.

Os fatores que ajudam a desencadear a depressão podem ir desde separações, traumas de infância, traumas provocados por doenças graves até o uso de **drogas**, levando à dependência química; entre os variados sintomas alguns são mais frequentes e comuns a todos os pacientes.

Os sintomas mais comuns da depressão são a tristeza constante, ideias suicidas, insegurança, angústias e medos infundados. Pode haver também irritabilidade, cansaço, pressões sociais, sono irregular com grande sonolência durante o dia e insônia à noite e **desinteresse** total pela vida.

Em casos mais graves de depressão, algumas pessoas perdem o emprego, abandonam os estudos e se excluem de seu círculo social, vivendo à margem de tudo e de todos, costumam ter manias de perseguição, achando que tudo à sua volta oferece grande perigo e que sempre é o alvo.

Após aprender tudo isso, Marina quis saber da médica qual seria o tratamento para a depressão. Ela explicou que consiste na **combinação** de antidepressivos e psicoterapia, um trabalho feito em parceria entre um psiquiatra e um psicólogo e que era muito importante frisar que os medicamentos só poderiam ser adquiridos com a receita médica em mãos.

Marina entendeu a diferença entre tristeza e depressão. Compreendeu melhor por que muitas mulheres estão sofrendo bruscamente essa doença. Buscou informações sobre o tratamento da depressão no Brasil. Foi um grande aprendizado.

No período de licença médica do trabalho, Marina conheceu Fabrício no hospital, um médico pediatra especialista em câncer infantil. Foi amor à primeira vista. Fabrício era um cavalheiro, um homem doce e preocupado com as pessoas ao seu redor, além de ótimo profissional, reconhecido por seu trabalho.

Marina, que tinha problemas para se sentir bem com a vida, se cobrava muito, não suportava mudanças e, além disso, tinha tido problemas de saúde por causa do **estresse**. Ela percebeu que havia muito a ser feito pelo próximo, por aqueles que sofrem desde muito cedo e passam, muitas vezes, a vida inteira lutando em um hospital.

Marina melhorou, estava curada graças ao apoio de sua amiga Adriana que a ajudou nesse momento importante, sem falar também na equipe médica que a assistiu.

Adriana deu-lhe conselhos para mudar seus **hábitos**, conscientizando-a da importância de se sentir bem consigo mesma, não ser tão exigente e não ter medo de mudanças. A importância de ter bons amigos e profissionais dedicados é fundamental, é para toda a vida.

Resumo da história

Marina é uma profissional de sucesso no ramo do ensino, mais especificamente física voltada para a aviação. Após uma mudança em sua vida, encontra uma amiga de longa data e ambas resolvem colocar a conversa em dia. Após o encontro, porém, as coisas na vida de Marina passam a mudar de maneira inesperada, o que a leva a um quadro de depressão e redescobrimento.

Summary of the story

Marina is a successful professional in the field of teaching, more specifically physical aviation. After a change in her life, she meets a long-time friend, and both decide to catch up. After the meeting, however, things in Marina's life change unexpectedly, which leads to a chart of depression and rediscovery.

Vocabulary

- **física:** physics
- **concurso:** Entrance exams (for public service)
- **aeronáutica:** air force
- **respeitada:** respected
- **abstração:** abstraction
- **disciplina:** subject
- **matéria:** theme
- **dever:** duty
- **aviação:** aviation
- **mecânica:** mechanics
- **ministrará:** will teach
- **organizada:** organized
- **perfeccionista:** perfectionist
- **apaixonado:** in love
- **formaram:** graduated
- **antecedência:** in advance
- **agenda:** schedule
- **quanto tempo!:** long time, no see!
- **emprego:** job
- **demorar um pouco:** to take a while
- **besteira:** nonsense
- **orgulhoso:** proud
- **sozinha:** alone
- **assunto:** matter
- **paciência:** patience
- **graças a Deus:** thank God
- **estômago:** stomach
- **funcionário:** employee
- **bolsa:** purse
- **cartomante:** fortune teller
- **pena:** pity
- **lecionar:** to teach
- **outrora:** formerly
- **preocupada:** worried
- **especializado:** specialized
- **desdobrar:** to make an effort
- **dono do apartamento:** landlord
- **comprador:** buyer
- **estafa:** fatigue
- **depressão:** depression
- **relacionamento:** relationship
- **saudável:** healthy
- **inescrupuloso:** unscrupulous
- **mudanças:** changes
- **psicóloga:** psychologist
- **sociedade:** society
- **negativo:** bad

- **sistema nervoso central:** central nervous system
- **competitividade:** competitiveness
- **drogas:** drugs
- **desinteresse:** disinterest
- **combinação:** mix
- **estresse:** stress
- **hábitos:** habits

Questions about the story

1. **Qual a profissão de Marina?**

   a) Aviadora
   b) Engenheira
   c) Física
   d) Professora

2. **Que características descrevem Marina?**

   a) Organizada e perfeccionista
   b) Inteligente e sagaz
   c) Rápida e prática
   d) Calma e serena

3. **De onde Marina conhece sua melhor amiga?**

   a) Faculdade
   b) Escola
   c) Trabalho
   d) Bairro

4. **Qual foi a primeira mudança na vida de Marina?**

   a) Mudança de turmas
   b) Saída do apartamento
   c) Pedido de casamento
   d) Depressão

5. **Com quem Marina foi morar após o término de seu relacionamento?**

   a) Sozinha em um novo apartamento
   b) Com seus pais
   c) Com sua amiga
   d) Com um novo namorado

Answers

1. D
2. A
3. B
4. A
5. C

CHAPTER NINE

INDEFINITE PRONOUNS

Vida saudável, alimente esta ideia – Healthy life, feed this idea

Lúcio Silva desde pequeno leva uma vida **saudável**. Para ele, estar com boa saúde é muito importante para **viver** bem. Quando **criança**, Lúcio aprendeu a se alimentar corretamente, pois seus pais sempre faziam **refeições** com **verduras** e **legumes** e preparavam **suco** natural da fruta para acompanhar o almoço, os lanches e o jantar.

Com o passar dos anos, Lúcio começou a praticar esportes. Ele ia **frequentemente** à **academia** e quase sempre participava de competições de **natação** e vôlei, seus esportes preferidos.

Atualmente, Lúcio tem 32 anos e apresenta um bom estilo físico. Ainda hoje, ele mantém os antigos hábitos. Gosta de **manter** seu estilo de vida saudável, aprendeu quando criança e agora faz o possível para se manter bem. Não é de **ferro**; às vezes, tem vontade de comer algo diferente e acaba não resistindo a um chocolate, mas não deixa que isso vire rotina. Tenha certeza, você **raramente** o verá parado, pois está sempre fazendo alguma coisa.

Lúcio se formou em nutrição e tornou-se um nutricionista **renomado** em sua cidade. Já salvou **inúmeras** vidas de pessoas com **transtornos** alimentares como **bulimia** e situações de subnutrição.

O currículo de Lúcio é extenso. Já foi nutricionista no **exército**, atendeu em clínicas particulares, participou da organização Médicos sem Fronteiras onde cuidou de crianças subnutridas, salvando muitas vidas. Também trabalhou em hospitais públicos na cidade onde morava, ajudando a população mais **carente**.

Também era professor em uma faculdade de nutrição e muito **exigente**, fazia tudo para que os alunos aprendessem de verdade, pois acreditava no fato de que precisamos de profissionais sérios e não de nutricionistas que inventam dietas da moda que muito **prometem** e nada cumprem, **enganando** os pacientes ou ainda dietas muito distantes da condição de vida dos clientes.

Lúcio insistia em passar **boas práticas** de alimentação saudável a seus alunos e pacientes, como ingerir muita **água** para deixar o corpo **hidratado** e não sobrecarregar os **rins**; comer alimentos ricos em fibras; fazer de alimentos *in natura* ou minimamente processados a base da alimentação; utilizar óleos, **gorduras**, sal e **açúcar** em pequenas **quantidades** ao temperar e cozinhar alimentos; limitar o consumo de alimentos processados e evitar o de alimentos ultra processados.

Na opinião de Lúcio, as práticas de boa alimentação deveriam ser melhor difundidas pelo Ministério da Saúde e **veículos de informação** e todas as pessoas deveriam ser **instruídas** a optar por diferentes tipos de alimentos, como os *in natura*, que são essencialmente partes de plantas ou de animais, por exemplo, carnes, verduras, legumes e frutas.

Lúcio também indica os alimentos minimamente processados, aqueles que não envolvem agregação de substâncias ao alimento original, como limpeza, moagem e pasteurização. São essencialmente arroz, feijão, lentilhas, cogumelos, frutas secas e sucos de frutas sem adição de açúcar ou outras substâncias; castanhas e nozes sem sal ou açúcar; farinhas de mandioca, de milho de tapioca ou de **trigo** e massas frescas.

Ele sempre diz que um nutricionista não **aconselha** o uso de alimentos processados, pois são fabricados pela indústria com a adição de sal ou açúcar a alimentos para torná-los duráveis e mais palatáveis e atraentes, como por exemplo, conservas em salmoura (cenoura, pepino, ervilhas, palmito); compotas de frutas; carnes salgadas e defumadas; sardinha e **atum** de latinha, queijos e pães.

E não precisa nem dizer que os alimentos ultra processados são abominados na área da saúde, não é mesmo? Claro, são formulações industriais, em sua maioria, com pouco ou nenhum alimento inteiro e contém **aditivos** como, por exemplo, salsichas, biscoitos, geleias, sorvetes, chocolates, molhos, misturas para bolo, "barras energéticas", sopas, macarrão e temperos "instantâneos", "chips", refrigerantes, produtos **congelados** e prontos para aquecimento como **massas**, pizzas, hambúrgueres e *nuggets*. Ou seja, estes alimentos são substâncias comestíveis, com pouco ou nenhum benefício à saúde. Pelo contrário, é possível que façam algum malefício ao paciente com tantos produtos **químicos** adicionados.

A **batalha** de Lúcio era mesmo para desmistificar as dietas milagrosas que enganavam muitas pessoas e não traziam nenhuma melhora significativa. Ele passava os conhecimentos que tinha e esperava ver alguma mudança ao seu redor.

Incomodado ao observar que seu **sobrinho** e as outras crianças ao invés de comerem um lanche **equilibrado**, no dia a dia, levavam e compravam, na escola, salgadinhos e doces, Lúcio teve a certeza de que era hora de **agir**.

Assim, ele resolveu falar com o **diretor** sobre o problema e elaborou um projeto nutricional para apresentar à escola, conscientizando, dessa forma, os alunos de todas as **séries** do colégio estadual da cidade mineira onde morou, um município de 13 mil habitantes, sobre a importância da alimentação correta para uma vida saudável.

Os alunos tinham dificuldades para se alimentar bem. Gostavam de frituras, balinhas, pirulitos, chicletes e doces o tempo todo. Nesse momento, foi feito o projeto sobre alimentação saudável, balanceada e colorida, dando uma grande contribuição em relação ao crescimento e bem-estar desses alunos.

Para **estimular** a descoberta de sabores, Lúcio pediu que as professoras pudessem fazer piqueniques com a criançada. Sobre a **toalha** estendida no pátio da escola, frutas, sucos naturais, água e biscoitos com cereais.

Tanto Lúcio quanto os professores dos estudantes ficaram muitos satisfeitos com os resultados do projeto. Os pais estavam satisfeitos com a mudança na alimentação dos alunos e ficaram mais **empolgados** ainda quando souberam que poderiam ajudar na **horta** escolar, uma extensão do primeiro projeto, em que as hortaliças e legumes plantados seriam aproveitados pela cantina na merenda escolar.

Ficou satisfeito e realizado quando o pai de um aluno revelou, durante uma reunião, que o projeto causara **mudança** na alimentação do filho que entendeu a importância dos nutrientes do **feijão** em seu **organismo** e começou a **diversificar** mais o prato, comendo inclusive, o feijão do qual antes não gostava.

Lúcio sabia que a mudança na alimentação iria beneficiar seu sobrinho e também as outras crianças da escola, assim como aconteceu com ele em sua **infância**. Ele também sabia que uma alimentação adequada evita estresse, nervosismo, deixa as crianças menos ansiosas e mais motivadas.

Buscou também reunir-se com os pais e **funcionários** da escola para dar uma **palestra** sobre o assunto. Não adiantava mudar a alimentação apenas na escola, as famílias também precisavam saber, para que a mudança fosse completa.

A vida da população brasileira não era tão saudável, mas poderia melhorar e muito. Não só a prática de **exercícios**, mas a alimentação era o mais importante. Quem não tem condições de pagar uma academia, pode fazer uma caminhada ou **corrida** na rua, fazer exercícios no parque, por exemplo.

Lúcio preparou um pequeno resumo com sugestões de mudança e entregou a todos os participantes da palestra. Quatro recomendações principais que devem ser levadas em conta antes de qualquer refeição:

Alimentos *in natura* ou minimamente processados devem ser a base da alimentação.

Óleos, gorduras, sal e açúcar devem ser utilizados em pequenas quantidades durante o preparo dos alimentos.

O uso de alimentos processados deve ser limitado a pequenas quantidades, como ingredientes de preparações culinárias, ou parte das refeições com base em alimentos *in natura* ou minimante processados.

Evite alimentos ultra processados.

Quatro sugestões de **substituição** por alimentos mais saudáveis:

Pão de forma por tapioca, bolo de milho caseiro, cuscuz, pão de queijo ou bolo de mandioca caseiro.

Macarrão instantâneo por massas feitas apenas de farinha e água.

Trocar salgadinhos de milho por frutas frescas ou secas e castanhas ou nozes ou biscoitos caseiros.

Trocar maionese por iogurte natural ou queijo cottage caseiro, pesto, maionese de banana verde, de cenoura, etc.

Trocar Cereais matinais por amaranto em flocos, aveia em flocos grandes ou granola caseira. Trocar caldos e temperos por ervas naturais.

O desafio de Lúcio era mostrar às pessoas que ter uma vida saudável é mais do que ter um corpo saudável. Viver desta maneira inclui diversos aspectos relacionados ao modo como vivemos: Depende da cultura, da **crença**, dos valores que compartilhamos com a comunidade em que fomos criados. Essa combinação de aspectos individuais e coletivos, associada a fatores como as reações emocionais (estresse, nervosismo, medo, tranquilidade, alegria, entusiasmo) nos mostra o quanto é complexo pensar a saúde e falar de um estilo de vida saudável. Ele sabia que ninguém é igual a ninguém e que nenhuma família seria idêntica.

A comunidade da escola ficou muito contente com a atitude de Lúcio e se sentiram especiais com toda a atenção dada a eles. É claro que não mudaram totalmente seus hábitos alimentares, mas fizeram melhorias significativas. Lúcio teve a sensação de dever cumprido e continuava levando conhecimento aos outros.

Resumo da história

Lúcio foi acostumado desde pequeno a uma vida e alimentação saudáveis. Quando adulto, dedicou sua vida a esse objetivo, tornando-se nutricionista. A importância que Lúcio via na alimentação era tanta, que resolveu fazer uso de seus conhecimentos para ajudar a comunidade, começando por propor um novo plano alimentar para a escola de seu sobrinho.

Summary of the story

Lucio was accustomed from a young age to a healthy life and diet. As an adult, he dedicated his life to this goal by becoming a nutritionist. The importance that Lucio saw in food was so great that he decided to make use of his knowledge to help the community, starting by proposing a new diet plan for his nephew's school.

Vocabulary

- **saudável:** healthy
- **viver:** to live
- **criança:** child
- **refeições:** meals
- **verduras:** plants
- **legumes:** vegetables
- **suco:** juice
- **frequentemente:** often
- **academia:** gym
- **natação:** swimming
- **manter:** to keep
- **ferro:** steel
- **raramente:** rarely
- **renomado:** renowned
- **inúmeras:** countless
- **transtornos:** disorders
- **bulimia:** bulimia
- **exército:** army
- **carente:** in need
- **exigente:** demanding
- **prometem:** promise
- **enganado:** fooled
- **boas práticas:** good habits
- **água:** water
- **hidratado:** hydrated
- **rins:** kidneys
- **gorduras:** fat
- **açúcar:** sugar
- **quantidades:** amounts
- **veículos de informação:** media
- **instruídas:** taught
- **trigo:** wheat
- **aconselha:** advise
- **atum:** tuna
- **aditivos:** additions
- **congelados:** frozen
- **massa:** pasta
- **químicos:** chemical
- **batalha:** battle
- **sobrinho:** nephew
- **equilibrado:** balanced
- **agir:** to act
- **diretor:** director
- **séries:** grades
- **estimular:** to stimulate
- **toalha:** towel
- **empolgados:** excited
- **horta:** vegetable garden
- **mudança:** change
- **feijão:** beans
- **organismo:** organism
- **diversificar:** to diversify
- **infância:** childhood
- **funcionários:** employees

- **palestra:** lecture
- **exercícios:** exercises
- **corrida:** running
- **substituição:** replacement
- **crença:** belief

Questions about the story

1. **Quando Lúcio teve seu primeiro contato com a alimentação saudável?**

   a) Na faculdade
   b) Na infância
   c) Após seu casamento
   d) Quando já idoso

2. **Em qual profissão Lúcio se formou?**

   a) Medicina
   b) Nutrição
   c) Educação Física
   d) Fisioterapia

3. **Qual foi a proposta de Lúcio para a escola?**

   a) Fechar a cantina
   b) Que os alunos trouxessem comida de casa
   c) Oferecer alimentação saudável
   d) Aumentar o preço dos produtos

4. **Na opinião de Lúcio, quem deveria comunicar boas práticas em saúde?**

   a) Os professores
   b) Os pais
   c) O Ministério da Saúde
   d) As prefeituras

5. **Qual tipo de alimento deveria ser evitado?**

   a) Ultra processados
   b) *In natura*
   c) Integrais
   d) Orgânicos

Answers

1. B
2. B
3. C
4. C
5. A

CHAPTER TEN

DIRECT AND INDIRECT DISCOURSE

Não acredito em você, mas... – I don't believe in you but...

Carlos é um **engenheiro** de software que trabalha na grande São Paulo. Casado, tem filhos, e vive entre a casa e o trabalho. Trabalha demais, está **constantemente** preso no **trânsito** e muito **cansado**.

A empresa em que trabalha é uma multinacional e as **demandas** de trabalho são crescentes. É impossível não ficar desanimado às vezes, mas isso tem relação direta com a crise brasileira, com as tensões entre EUA e Coreia do Norte, com a situação na Venezuela, com o **Oriente Médio** ou com o grande mistério da existência humana.

Carlos se sente preso, falta **ânimo** em sua vida. É como se trabalhar 44 horas semanais **sugasse** suas **energias**. Ele não tem tempo para os filhos, para a **esposa**, não conseguia fazer atividades físicas ou viagens mais longas com a família. Não lhe sobrava tempo para ler um livro que não fosse da sua área de trabalho ou ir ao cinema com Cintia, sua esposa há 15 anos. O máximo que lhe sobrara era um *happy hour* com o pessoal do trabalho uma sexta-feira ou outra, para **aliviar** o estresse.

Era **compreensível**, sua família o **entendia**, apesar de sua esposa ser **ciumenta**. Os filhos já estavam acostumados com a rotina do pai e faziam mais atividades com a mãe, que trabalhava menos e também conviviam com a **empregada**.

Ok. Carlos até poderia ter mais tempo se **administrasse** mais o seu próprio horário, mas sua rotina executiva estressante o impedia de pensar por este lado. Ele **preferia** inventar alguma desculpa para não ser mais saudável ou para não deixar de fumar, mas não passavam de aflições de uma classe média, seus amigos passavam por situações **parecidas**.

Ele estava saindo do trabalho e pegando o **trânsito** para voltar para casa como sempre fazia, com a mesma rotina de sempre, todos os dias no mesmo horário.

Apesar das especulações da esposa, Carlos era um marido **fiel** e vivia se **esquivando** das **secretárias** de onde trabalhava. Ele não dava motivos, era um homem sério, cansado e um pouco **preguiçoso**. E além do mais, sua esposa era linda, a melhor mulher que poderia **aguentar** uma rotina tão cansativa ao seu lado. Ele sabia disso, pois já tinha um ou outro cabelo branco na cabeça.

Carlos tinha 38 anos, com essa idade ele já tinha perdido as **esperanças** de ser um **executivo** milionário fechando negócios em Jacarta, com maletas cheias de dólares. Poderia apenas tentar a sorte jogando na **loteria** ou, no máximo, virando um *youtuber*, o que ele não faria, pois era muito sério. Certo dia, pensando na vida, distraído enquanto dirigia, o **pneu** do seu carro fura e Carlos é obrigado a encostar e esperar pelo guincho. Ele não queria se **sujar** e estava cansado, digo, preguiçoso demais para suar trocando o pneu.

Decidiu sair do carro e **fumar** um cigarro. Mal sabia ele que essa ação lhe custaria caro. Após dois cigarros e algumas **ligações** para localizar o guincho, um carro para e oferece **ajuda**, Carlos agradece, mas recusa, dizendo que o guincho já está a caminho.

Para sua surpresa, os dois homens o rendem e anunciam o **assalto**. Levam tudo o que podem, inclusive o **celular**, a **carteira**, a **aliança** de ouro e o **escapulário** de prata que ganhou de sua mãe e fogem deixando Carlos e o carro lá.

Carlos entra em desespero, não sabe o que fazer. O mais prudente seria esperar o guincho, mas ele não tinha mais como **provar** que era ele mesmo, estava sem o cartão da **seguradora**, o gps do localizador da seguradora funcionava pelo celular que agora estava com os bandidos, ele sequer poderia ligar para contatar alguém, sentia-se perdido. Tentou **pedir carona**, mas as pessoas torciam o nariz e iam embora. Claro, hoje em dia é difícil **acreditar** em alguém, as pessoas andam com **medo**.

Resolveu **trancar** o carro e foi embora **andando** e pedindo carona. Em certo momento, parou uma **caminhonete**.

— Está indo para onde, amigão? Todo bem vestido assim andando na pista, está precisando de algo?

— Cara, você não vai acreditar, fui assaltado, meu carro está quebrado no **acostamento** da BR a mais ou menos uma meia hora daqui. Preciso de uma carona até algum lugar perto de casa, se você puder me ajudar.

— Claro, sobe aí.

O homem viajava com seu filho e ficou com pena e **abismado** com a história que Carlos contou. E os três foram conversando o caminho todo. O filho tinha uma caixa de **isopor** com cervejas e ofereceu uma para Carlos, que aceitou para aliviar o estresse, já que não podia fumar no carro. Eles ficaram com pena e deixaram Carlos em casa, apesar de terem se desviado bastante de sua rota. O homem lhe deu um cartão pra contato e lhe desejou boa **sorte**.

Carlos interfonou e entrou em casa abatido e todo amarrotado.

— Você não sabe o que aconteceu...

— O quê?

— Uma coisa horrível.

— Para de enrolar, Carlos! O que foi? Você chega uma hora dessas e com essa cara.

— Fui assaltado! Levaram tudo.

— Não acredito!

— Olhe. Levam o celular, a carteira, nossa aliança... tudo.

— Como assim? **Onde**?

E ele contou tudo, tudo exatamente como aconteceu. O pneu, a espera, o guincho, o cigarro, o assalto, a ajuda.

— Que coisa, hein?! – disse Cintia, com ar debochado.

— E que culpa eu tenho?

— **Nenhuma**. Você não tem culpa de nada.

— Pois é. Hoje em...

— SEU **mentiroso**!

— Quê?

— Você acha que sou idiota? Uma **palhaça**? Você chega aqui cheirando a bebida, todo amassado, uma hora dessas e acha que vou acreditar nessa mentira?

— O rapaz me deu uma cerveja, qual é o problema?

— Onde você estava?? Não mente para mim! Você nunca chega uma hora dessas! Nunca bebe no meio da semana, o que está acontecendo? Você só pode ter tirado essa aliança para estar com alguma mulher biscate por aí. O que foi? Ela te embebedou e te roubou? Agora volta pra casa com essa cara lavada dizendo essas **mentiras** e quer que eu acredite?

— Mas, amor eu estou falando a verdade...

— Você vai insistir nisso? Eu já falei que não acredito em você. Deve ter esquecido essa aliança no motel, não é mesmo? Seu **hipócrita**!

— Amor, eu não sei o que dizer. Eu chego aqui falando a verdade e você me **acusa** de uma coisa dessas?

— Ah, não sabe o que dizer? Não tente virar a situação. Por que você não me ligou então? Para avisar que o carro estava no prego? Ah, devia estar ocupado demais para me fazer uma ligação, não é mesmo?!

— Eu esqueci!! Eu liguei pro guincho e esperei, foi isso que eu fiz.

— Ah, esqueceu? Você deveria ter pensado em uma desculpa melhor, Carlos! Eu detesto mentira!

— Mas eu não estou mentindo!

— Eu não acredito em você.

Nada do que Carlos falasse a **convenceria**. Cintia estava cega de ciúmes, saiu de casa, levou as crianças e não quis saber de papo. Deve ter ido para a casa da mãe ou algum outro lugar. Ela queria punir Carlos, que não entendia o porquê de ela estar assim. Não era a primeira vez que Cintia fazia isso, dar **escândalo** por situações **desnecessárias** e depois pedir desculpas.

Carlos saiu. Foi andando à **delegacia** fazer um boletim de ocorrência. Talvez com esse documento ela acreditasse nele. Também ligou para o guincho e resolveu a questão do carro. Por último, ligou para o seu melhor amigo, Júnior, que foi correndo encontrá-lo e escutar toda a história.

...

— É, amigão, e foi isso. Você acredita?

— Acredito, Carlos! Totalmente compreensível. Para mim, que sou seu amigo, não sua esposa. Cara, **mulheres** são difíceis de entender, mas dê um tempo a ela, para colocar a cabeça no lugar e perceber que exagerou e não te escutou, não acreditou em você. Depois você conversa com ela direito, mostra o boletim de ocorrência e diz que ela não precisa fazer esse escândalo todo sempre que algo diferente da rotina de vocês acontecer.

— É, você está certo, toda vez que algo na rotina muda ela acha estranho. Talvez a culpa seja minha que faço tudo igual sempre. Preciso mudar isto **urgentemente**. Na verdade, preciso mudar muitas coisas em minha vida, meus hábitos, meus horários, toda essa situação. Sinto que não tenho controle sobre nada, estou apenas vivendo como se não pudesse escolher.

— Então a parte mais difícil já passou. Você já sabe o que precisa fazer, agora é só pôr em prática.

Naquele dia, Carlos decidiu que dali em diante não teria mais apenas uma rotina.

Resumo da história

Carlos era um homem de negócios que trabalhava muito e isso fazia com que não tivesse muito tempo para sua família e para si próprio, o que causava desconforto em sua esposa. Em um dia de infortúnio, Carlos enfrentou uma situação que alterou sua rotina, causando os ciúmes de sua esposa e lhe trazendo inúmeros problemas.

Summary of the story

Carlos was a business man who worked hard, and because of that he did not have much time for his family and for himself, which caused discomfort in his wife. On a day of misfortune, Carlos faced a situation that changed his routine, causing the jealousy of his wife and bringing him various problems.

Vocabulary

- **engenheiro:** engineer
- **constantemente:** constantly
- **trânsito:** traffic
- **cansado:** tired
- **demandas:** requests
- **Oriente Médio:** Middle East
- **ânimo:** stamina
- **sugasse:** absorb
- **energias:** energies
- **esposa:** wife
- **aliviar:** to relieve
- **compreensível:** understandable
- **entendia:** understand
- **ciumenta:** jealous
- **empregada:** maid
- **administrasse:** administer
- **preferia:** would rather
- **parecidas:** similar
- **fiel:** loyal
- **esquivando:** avoiding
- **secretárias:** secretaries
- **preguiçoso:** lazy
- **aguentar:** to bear
- **esperanças:** hope
- **executivo:** business man
- **loteria:** lottery
- **pneu:** tire
- **sujar:** to get dirty
- **fumar:** to smoke
- **ligações:** calls
- **ajuda:** help
- **assalto:** robbery
- **celular:** cell phone
- **carteira:** wallet
- **aliança:** wedding ring
- **escapulário:** scapular
- **provar:** to prove
- **seguradora:** insurance company
- **pedir carona**: to ask for a lift
- **acreditar:** to believe
- **medo:** fear
- **trancar:** to lock
- **andando:** walking
- **caminhonete:** pickup truck
- **acostamento:** road block
- **abismado:** astounded
- **isopor:** styrofoam
- **sorte:** luck
- **onde:** where
- **nenhuma:** none

- **mentiroso:** liar
- **palhaça:** clown
- **mentiras:** lies
- **hipócrita:** hypocrite
- **acusa:** accuse
- **covenceria:** would convince
- **escândalo:** scandal
- **desnecessárias:** unnecessary
- **delegacia:** police station
- **mulheres:** women
- **urgentemente:** urgently

Questions about the story

1. **Em que cidade Carlos trabalha?**
   a) São Paulo
   b) Rio de Janeiro
   c) Brasília
   d) Salvador
2. **Como Carlos costumava chegar ao trabalho?**
   a) Metrô
   b) Ônibus
   c) Carro
   d) Carona
3. **O que Carlos estava fazendo no momento do assalto?**
   a) Jogando no celular
   b) Fumando
   c) Ligando para sua esposa
   d) Tentando trocar o pneu
4. **Como Carlos conseguiu chegar em sua casa?**
   a) Esperou pelo seguro do carro
   b) Ligou para um amigo
   c) Pegou transporte público
   d) Conseguiu uma carona
5. **Qual foi a reação de sua esposa?**
   a) Ficou preocupada com o ocorrido
   b) Ficou brava por Carlos não tê-la avisado
   c) Não acreditou na história
   d) Ajudou Carlos com a papelada do seguro

Answers

1. A
2. C
3. B
4. D
5. C

CONCLUSION

Hello again, reader!

We hope you've enjoyed our stories and the way we've presented them. Each chapter, as you will have noticed, was a way to practice a language tool which you will regularly use when speaking Portuguese. Whether it's Verbs, Pronouns or Simple Conversations, the Portuguese tongue has a great essence of grammar which can be just as challenging to learn as it can be entertaining.

Never forget: learning a language doesn't *have* to be a boring activity if you find the proper way to do it. Hopefully we've provided you with a hands-on, fun way to expand your knowledge in Portuguese and you can apply your lessons to future ventures.

Feel free to use this book further ahead when you need to go back to remembering vocabulary and expressions — in fact, we encourage it.

Believe in yourself and never be ashamed to make mistakes. Even the best can fall; it's those who get up that can achieve greatness! Take care!

PS: Keep an eye out for more books like this one; we're not done teaching you Portuguese! Head over to www.LingoMastery.com and read our free articles, sign up for our newsletter and check out our Youtube channel. We give away so much free stuff that will accelerate your Portuguese learning and you don't want to miss that!

Take care and until next time!

MORE BOOKS BY LINGO MASTERY

Have you been trying to learn Portuguese and simply can't find the way to expand your vocabulary?

Do your teachers recommend you boring textbooks and complicated stories that you don't really understand?

Are you looking for a way to learn the language quicker without taking shortcuts?

If you answered "Yes!" to at least one of those previous questions, then this book is for you! We've compiled the **2000 Most Common Words in Portuguese**, a list of terms that will expand your vocabulary to levels previously unseen.

Did you know that — according to an important study — learning the top two thousand (2000) most frequently used words will enable you to understand up to **84%** of all non-fiction and **86.1%** of fiction literature and **92.7%** of oral speech? Those are amazing stats, and this book will take you even further than those numbers!

In this book:

- A detailed introduction with tips and tricks on how to improve your learning
- A list of 2000 of the most common words in Portuguese and their translations
- An example sentence for each word – in both Portuguese and English
- Finally, a conclusion to make sure you've learned and supply you with a final list of tips

Don't look any further, we've got what you need right here!

In fact, we're ready to turn you into a Portuguese speaker... are you ready to get involved in becoming one?

Do you know what the hardest thing for a Portuguese learner is?

Finding PROPER reading material that they can handle...which is precisely the reason we've written this book!

Teachers love giving out tough, expert-level literature to their students, books that present many new problems to the reader and force them to search for words in a dictionary every five minutes — it's not entertaining, useful or motivating for the student at all, and many soon give up on learning at all!

In this book we have compiled 20 easy-to-read, compelling and fun stories that will allow you to expand your vocabulary and give you the tools to improve your grasp of the wonderful Portuguese tongue.

How Portuguese Short Stories for Beginners works:

- Each story is interesting and entertaining with realistic dialogues and day-to-day situations.
- The summaries follow a synopsis in Portuguese and in English of what you just read, both to review the lesson and for you to see if you understood what the tale was about.
- At the end of those summaries, you'll be provided with a list

of the most relevant vocabulary involved in the lesson, as well as slang and sayings that you may not have understood at first glance!

- Finally, you'll be provided with a set of tricky questions in Portuguese, providing you with the chance to prove that you learned something in the story. Don't worry if you don't know the answer to any — we will provide them immediately after, but no cheating!
- We want you to feel comfortable while learning the tongue; after all, no language should be a barrier for you to travel around the world and expand your social circles!

So look no further! Pick up your copy of Portuguese Short Stories for Beginners and start learning Portuguese right now!

This book has been written by a native Brazilian author and is recommended for A2+ level learners.

Is conversational Portuguese turning a little too tricky for you? Do you have *no idea* how to order a meal or book a room at a hotel?

If your answer to any of the previous questions was *'Yes',* then this book is for you!

If there's even been something tougher than learning the grammar rules of a new language, it's finding the way to speak with other people in that tongue. Any student knows this – we can try our best at practicing, but you always want to avoid making embarrassing mistakes or not getting your message through correctly.

'How do I get out of this situation?' many students ask themselves, to no avail, but no answer is forthcoming.

Until now.

We have compiled **MORE THAN ONE HUNDRED** conversational Portuguese stories for beginners along with their translations, allowing new Portuguese speakers to have the necessary tools to begin studying how to set a meeting, rent a car or tell a doctor that they don't feel well. We're not wasting time here with conversations that don't go anywhere: if you want to know how to solve problems (while learning a ton of Portuguese along the way, obviously), this book is for you!

How Conversational Portuguese Dialogues works:

- Each new chapter will have a fresh, new story between two people who wish to solve a common, day-to-day issue that you will surely encounter in real life.
- An Portuguese version of the conversation will take place first, followed by an English translation. This ensures that you fully understood just what it was that they were saying.
- Before and after the main section of the book, we shall provide you with an introduction and conclusion that will offer you important strategies, tips and tricks to allow you to get the absolute most out of this learning material.
- That's about it! Simple, useful and incredibly helpful; you will **NOT** need another conversational Portuguese book once you have begun reading and studying this one!

We want you to feel comfortable while learning the tongue; after all, no language should be a barrier for you to travel around the world and expand your social circles!

So look no further! Pick up your copy of **Conversational Portuguese Dialogues** and start learning Portuguese *right now*!

Please notice that this book has been written with a Brazilian Portuguese touch.

Made in the USA
Middletown, DE
11 November 2020

23739714R00076